Overcoming Organizational Myopia

Breaking Through Siloed Organizations

John Knotts

ISBN-13: 978-1945151002
ISBN-10: 1945151005

Special discounts are available on quantity purchases by corporations, associations, educators, and others. For additional details, contact the author at the email address listed below.
John.Knotts@crossctr.com

DEDICATION

Many people can credit their parents for the way they are today. Mine have been a strong influence in my life as well. My father passed away in mid-2015 and we miss him very much. He was drafted in the Army and became a fireman and police officer when he separated from service. Over his many years on the force, he climbed to the position of Director of Public Safety. I am very proud of my father and think of him often.

To him, I dedicate this book. Miss you dad!

BUSINESS EXECUTIVE REVIEWS

This book was reviewed by several business leaders from industries including Healthcare, Fitness, Private Ventures, Technology, Business, Education, Oil and Gas, Military, Marketing, Nonprofit, and Insurance. Below are a few of these reviews.

*"The writing style in **Overcoming Organizational Myopia: Breaking Through Siloed Organizations** is easy to follow. Unlike some business books, this one is a quick read. It's clear that you're passionate about the subject."*

Jon Copulsky, MBA, Chief Marketing Officer, Northwestern University.

*"**Overcoming Organizational Myopia: Breaking Through Siloed Organizations** is exceptionally relevant to every organization I am a part of. It probably will be to you too. John Knotts does an exceptional job of not only diagnosing frustrating barriers to organizational effectiveness, but also bringing clear and concise solutions. After reading this book, the world at work will make a lot more sense, and leaders will be empowered to change. Reading this book is like getting corrective lenses for your organization's nearsightedness. I've really enjoyed reading your book."*

Brent Fessler, President, Hallmark University.

"Spectacular, powerful, and practical lessons learned, ready for immediate application in the private, public, Government, Military, and the NGOs sectors throughout the world!

You want to innovate. You want your organization to strive. You want your business to excel. Then, free yourself and them from the shackles of the organizational siloes. Relish the power of communication, cooperation, coordination, and collaboration (4Cs) to drive exponential growth and value creation.

*Applicable at all levels of the organization, John Knotts' book, **Overcoming Organizational Myopia**, is a spectacular leadership strategy, practical roadmap, and powerful management process designed to help you and your business analyze, navigate and break through the silos of the organization.*

Read this book, then read it again. Learn it, and apply it. It is the strategic, operational, and tactical weapon you and your organization should have to innovate, strive, and excel."

Grigor Bambekov, CLSS MBB, PMP; Director, Operational Services, Operational Excellence Management System, and Risk Management at Andeavor.

*"In his new book **Overcoming Organizational Myopia: Breaking Through Stovepipe Organizations**, John Knotts has written a book filled with simple, straightforward, common sense approaches to dealing with issues affecting operational excellence.*

Knotts does a good job of laying out his argument and the premises for the argument. He effectively describes his operational terms and their respective definitions, the underlying reasons for myopia and what he refers to as the creation of organizational siloes, and then laying the foundation for what Organizational Myopia (OM) is and what, then, can be done about it. I particularly liked his argument against the application of organization design and restructuring, used by so many management groups to treat the underlying problems associated with OM.

He uses a case study throughout to expose the elements of the argument and its related issues. Then connects it to an important principle in the Quality Improvement area - Deming's 14th point of breaking down barriers throughout the organization as a path to organizational effectiveness.

Following the laying out of his rationale for dealing with OM, he goes on to describe a set of action elements for dealing with it. I particularly liked how he set this up with a Table of Strategic and Organizational Methods for Dealing with OM as his introduction to the various methods of treatment.

He effectively uses this to introduce his preferred approach then identifies many of the underlying elements that contribute to OM, followed by what can reasonably be expected in terms of results and, as importantly, who the target audience is.

The remainder of the book is an elucidation of each of those methods and how each element of the target audience can use them. All-in-all, a logical and reasonable approach to dealing with an infectious problem that many organizations experience.

I think the book is well laid-out, logical in its flow, interesting to read and will be very useful to the reader."

Richard J. Buckles, Ph.D., Speaker, Author, International Consultant - Business Psychologist, and Executive Coach

"Ever wondered why, when Technology and Automation solutions have grown leaps and bounds, many organizations are still struggling to even survive. It should have been a no-brainer to turn around an organization that is failing in all fronts with Technology, Innovation, Customer Focus, etc., in their armoury.

But does adoption of technology and innovation alone solve an Organization's problem? Perhaps not! CEOs and bright young minds from some of the best institutions in the world still are finding it difficult to put a finger on the problem. Besides looking outward, looking inwards perhaps may help. When we meditate in India, we chant the mantra "OM" to focus and centre to go deep inside oneself.

I guess John Knotts' has now identified a similar mantra "OM" - Organizational Myopia--one that can be a tool for CEOs to centre themselves!

***Overcoming Organizational Myopia: Breaking Through Siloed Organizations**, is a fantastic primer for any CEO who wants to turn around her organization. Here, in this book,*

John gently guides a CEO to see where the rot is lurking. He lays out, backed by enormous experience, nine key areas, which, when unattended, leads to a typical rot in an organization.

John doesn't just talk of the source of the problem, but also prescribes the various steps to be taken to overcome OM. His book addresses both the Why and How of the challenges a CEO comes across, in a siloed organization. John goes beyond saying what is wrong.

Having had the good fortune to interact with many decision makers and having consulted with them from a Technology Solution perspective and in some cases not seeing any improvement subsequently, I firmly believe that the approach laid out by John will be a great help in steering an organization clear of OM.

I have worked with and known John for quite some time. John brings his vast experience and knowledge to the table in identifying and helping businesses solve issues. This book is a consolidation of all that experience.

This book is not just a must read but a must adopt and adapt for CEOs"

Vedantam Ayyangar, Assistant Vice President, Solutions / Pre-Sales, India

CONTENTS

FOREWORD

Joseph F. Paris, Jr.

☙ Author, "*State of Readiness*"
☙ Founder, Operational Excellence Society
☙ Founder, Readiness Institute

Joseph is an international entrepreneur and a sought-after strategist, consultant, mentor, and speaker with engagements around the world. Through his considerable experience, research, and articles written, he's become a world recognized "thought leader" on the subject of "Operational Excellence".

> *"John's storytelling*
> *brings to life the lessons and wisdom."*

*"John Knotts and his incredible book, **Overcoming Organizational Myopia: Breaking Through Siloed Organizations**, places the emphasis where it's needed -- focusing on the people, building a culture of leadership, and showing how an organization can operate better as an organization. He masterfully accomplishes this by illuminating the perils that must be avoided and the challenges that need to be overcome -- offering the reader insight and guidance on how to integrate an organization horizontally and not just optimize operations vertically within an organization's functional siloes.*

It's obvious that John understands that each of us is simultaneously a leader and a follower and that you can gauge the caliber of a leader by the caliber of those who follow. He also sets the expectation that it's easy to be assigned a title of leadership, but that a title does not make a person a leader -- that to become a leader takes a lot of time and effort to build the skills and, most important, to build the trust that is a necessary precursor to becoming a leader. After all, a leader is only a leader because people are willing -- wanting -- to follow.

The manner in which he delivers this incredible guidance is extremely effective. He offers a prescriptive approach but understands that each business faces its own unique set of circumstances and, rather than try to create a "one-size-fits-all" solution, John leaves it to the reader to adapt the lessons and guidance contained in the book to the unique business factors that they face. His use of storytelling connects the reader to real-life experiences and brings to life the amazing lessons and wisdom he's sharing. This approach is very effective and makes the book highly relatable to those who are responsible for ensuring a company becomes a high-performance organization.

*I'm 100% positive you'll find **Overcoming Organizational Myopia: Breaking Through Siloed Organizations** an easy and enjoyable read and you'll gain considerable insights, which you can put into action immediately; to the benefit of your company so that works better as a company -- and to the benefit of yourself to help you become a better leader!"*

PREFACE

Since 1998, I have worked in the field of consulting--either internal or external. Even earlier, I became involved in, what I now call operational excellence--about 1990 when the United States Air Force was adopting Total Quality Management.

Over the years I have witnessed organization after organization struggle to improve its operational excellence; often failing. Business statistics these days are terrible, and companies failing to bridge the gap between strategy and execution are seriously suffering. Let us look at the dismal statistics:

▸ Seventy percent of all strategic planning efforts fail

▸ Sixty percent of all organizational process improvement efforts fail

▸ Seventy percent of all change initiatives fail

▸ Seventy percent of workers are disengaged costing American businesses as much as $550 billion annually

One thing often resides at the heart of the problem--silos in an organization. Throughout my career, I have examined the myopia that can develop because of silos and discovered ways to overcome it.

ACKNOWLEDGMENTS

I have had a great many mentors--good and bad--who have helped me over the years. Some provided deeper insight into tactical approaches to problems. Others, inventive ways to tackle issues. The two best things I learned from all of them are: 1) There is never just one thing that needs to be addressed when dealing with an organization's issues (systems thinking); and 2) When faced with organizational issues, the root causes are always buried deep within the system and are never on the surface.

I also would like to express my deepest gratitude to my lovely wife, Lori. Without her help and support, this book would probably not have been possible.

Part 1
Introduction

Stan sits at the head of a small conference room table. His mind wanders as his branch chiefs around him relate their activities from the past week. Silvia, to his right, leads the financial management branch. She is efficient and effective and always makes sure the agency spends its money in ways she feels are wise.

Bill sits quietly across from Stan. He is reading email on his cellphone while Silvia discusses changes her branch decided to make to the travel expense approval process and outlines her plans to implement them next week. Bill runs the communications and computer support department. Everyone knows Bill wants to be the Chief Information Officer directly reporting to the agency director. As a branch chief, he constantly complains about a lack of manpower, but he feels certain that if he reported directly to the director, he would have adequate staff.

The meeting shifts to Pam, who leads the human resource department. Her latest gripe is that agency personnel are not keeping up with their annual safety training requirements and believes her office should not be responsible for ensuring everyone in the organization is trained. "It's their personal responsibility," she states.

As the weekly meeting drones on, Stan reflects on his past ten years with the agency. After eight years on the operations floor as a branch chief, he was promoted to this position as Support Division Chief. At the time, the director told him he wanted "someone running operations who had a connection to the agency's mission."

After he took the job, Stan quickly found out how little he knew about the support division of the agency. He believes all three of the branch chiefs: Sylvia, Bill and Pam, resent him for being promoted over them. They have done little to support him in the past two years.

The three were particularly upset when, immediately after assuming his new role, he cut the support staff by twenty percent and transferred the newly-vacated support positions to his old Operations Division. In Stan's mind, he was simply implementing changes to support the mission, as the director envisioned, and doing what it took to achieve the desired results.

In fact, over the last two years, he has further trimmed the support budget, so operations could have even more money to work with. In Stan's opinion, he was the best choice for this job. None of the others would have made the manpower and budget sacrifices he thought were clearly necessary and was willing to make.

Stan thinks about all he has accomplished, while considering that, in a few months, the chief position for the Operations Division will be coming open. Stan feels he is a great candidate for that role. He looks forward to the possibility of getting back into operations even though everything in operations changed when the director reorganized the two Operations Divisions into one last year.

Stan has been so removed from Operations' mission, he doesn't even know what it does anymore. He doesn't think that should matter though, because his experience from the last two years should make him a great candidate to solve Operations' problems. After all, look what he did for Support.

Does Stan's situation sound familiar?

Do you see anything wrong in this organization?

Have you ever worked for this type of organization?

Can you easily diagnose any problems you see here?

Better yet, how would you fix any problems you see?

Section 1
Book Content Overview

In the 1980s, Dr. Edwards Deming published a book, *"Out of Crisis,"* in which he introduced his Fourteen Points of Quality. This book provides a guide to the reader to apply Dr. Deming's now famous work; specifically, his 9th point that focused on breaking down barriers between staff areas. The 9th point of quality states: "Break down barriers between departments. People in research, design, sales, and production must work together as a team to foresee problems in production and in use that may be encountered with the product or service." Simply put, a fundamental principle of organizational effectiveness is to have all parts of the organization working together as a team.

Shortsighted organizations--those that fail to see the big picture or to have a strategic long-term vision--suffer from Organizational Myopia, or "OM". An organization suffering from OM is less effective or efficient at fulfilling its mission, or may be unable to do so at all. OM is successfully overcome by appropriately applying the strategic and organizational methods outlined in this book. Any organization; large, midsized, or even small, will be naturally susceptible to OM. And, most suffer from it. Unfortunately, the normal quick-fix methodologies often employed by leaders and managers to deal with OM usually result in ineffective short-term solutions and the organization returns to its OM behaviors.

How do you solve OM? A leader can take action to solve the negative effects of OM once he or she identifies them. But, successfully overcoming OM requires the consistent and systematic application of a full-spectrum of strategic and organizational improvement methods. To solve any problem, one must acknowledge and understand there is a problem, determine why it manifested, and act to correct it.

So, what is OM and how do you identify it? Myopia is a medical term for nearsightedness--also known as shortsightedness. People with myopia see near objects clearly but objects farther away appear blurred. Organizational Myopia occurs when the organization loses sight of its foundational purpose and its people and components become focused on their own short-sighted agendas. Like a person with Myopia, the short-sighted organization fails to see the big picture or have a long-term vision, causing its parts to no longer create a whole. In other words, the organization suffers from OM.

Organizations that suffer from OM are often referred to as "siloed" because the various parts of the organization do not look beyond their own silo and fail to focus on long-term organizational objectives. Military organizations refer to this kind of mentality as "being in a knife fight" or "being focused on the 25-meter target." Other terms used to describe OM are "empire building," "building sandboxes," "being close-knit," "a tight organization," or "operating in camps." As you can see, the organization's structure is a major factor that can influence the onset of OM. Consequently, you will often find the seeds of OM within the standard organization that is built with functional and divisional organizational structures.

Interestingly, it is a human tendency to naturally form into siloed groups. According to Abraham Maslow's Hierarchy of Needs, published in his book, *Motivation and Personality*, humans need to feel a sense of belonging and acceptance, regardless of whether that belonging and acceptance come from a large social group or small social connections. Maslow refers to this as the "Love and Belonging" layer in his hierarchy pyramid. Because of this, functional and divisional organizational structures tend to form strong silos rather quickly. However, all organizational structures form silos over time--it is a natural human phenomenon.

Frequently, in startup organizations, the small group of entrepreneurs who built the organization work closely together with a unified and understood purpose. At this point in the organization's development, most members are doing a little of everything to ensure the organization operates effectively. As the startup expands, the initial team evolves into separate specialized teams focused on different functions, such as sales, manufacturing, and delivery. Other functional specialties, such as human resources, information technology, and finance, develop to handle additional needs that arise as the operation grows. Silos automatically start to form as these teams develop within the organization. This is to be expected since, following Maslow's model, we naturally form into groups because of our need to belong.

According to Maslow, this need is so important that if it is not met, the individual cannot progress and grow to the "Esteem" and "Self-Actualization" layers in his hierarchy pyramid. Thus, the forming of silos in an organization is a result of the natural human desire to belong. It will happen. It cannot be stopped. And, it must occur for people to become more successful. Simply stated, humans need interaction to succeed and humans need silos to interact. It is when these silos become closed, fail to communicate with one another, and actually compete with other groups within the organization, that OM sets in.

OM has several ways of negatively impacting an organization. Often, in organizations that suffer from OM, people become so focused on local or group goals and standards, they lose sight of the overall goals and standards of the organization; undermining even a dedicated organization's efforts at transformation and renewal. OM also causes organizations to produce products and services that customers do not want, need, or ask for because the siloed groups fail to communicate with each other or with the customer to find out what he or she needs or expects. They often see themselves as the customer of their own process. Separated functions tend to focus on separate bottom-line objectives. For instance:

- ▶ The operational section that deals day-to-day with the customer and focuses on customer satisfaction
- ▶ The financial section focuses on the lowest cost operation

▶ The quality-control section focuses on producing the highest quality product possible

It is easy to see how these three functions, operating on their own within the organization, pull against one another and even cause each other to compete. Closed-group, siloed organizations typically suffer from a lack of interdepartmental communication. That lack of communication within the organization results in a lack of harmonized understanding among functional departments necessary to achieve the overall organizational goals.

A part of poor communication--hoarding of key information--can often occur within silos in organizations suffering from OM. Information hoarding leads to work delays, stalled progress, and even stoppages in production because functional departments are unable or unwilling to communicate and work together. Worse still, the departments are often not even aware of their information hoarding, the resulting action or inaction, or the impact of that action or inaction.

Because OM usually develops slowly through these closed silos and OM tends to shape or form the culture of an organization, little is done when, initially, silos within an organization build walls and become territorial. In fact, most organizations recognize functional specialization as necessary and important and encourage teams to build a siloed system.

Their inclination is correct! Without OM, silos are highly effective. Silos encourage competition between teams, leading to healthy and positive innovation. However, with OM, silos create an entrenched, myopic organization whose parts, or silos, do not work well together and fail to communicate.

Often, once leaders recognize OM, they take drastic measures to combat it, such as tearing down silos and creating an entirely new structure. This natural 'business' reaction to OM usually takes considerable time, is expensive and overly harsh. It is also typically a result of the frustration felt by the leader when he or she attempts to get the departments and teams to work together and finds they will not communicate. Restructuring or moving people around seems the only viable option to the leader. It is possible for this drastic organizational change to initially work. However, it is often only a temporary fix that results in an unproductive period followed by a return to the status quo of closed siloed groupings.

Consider that, even after the organizational structure is torn down, it is human nature for employees to rebuild the social networks they lost, re-form into similar social groups, and return to a siloed organization bent on OM. More importantly, following a drastic organizational change, employees *need* to re-form into these groups before the employees and the organization can effectively start performing again. Unfortunately, while the employees are flailing around trying to rebuild this "Love and Belonging" layer of Maslow's pyramid, they are generally less productive and successful at work.

Tearing down silos within an organization, in most cases, will not overcome the problems inherent with OM and will only create additional problems. Instead of these reactive measures, leaders should leverage strategic and organizational methods to overcome OM. To do so, they need to understand what OM is, diagnose the organization with OM, and identify the root causes of it.

As discussed, organizations, regardless of their structure, will always form into silos as a natural result of human nature. Having silos is actually good for an organization when the positive aspects of the functional specialization and divisional separation are leveraged, and the negative aspects are controlled. Functional specialization ensures strong personnel development, focus, and support. Divisional separation promotes honest and open competition between teams. This healthy and positive competition between teams leads to significant innovation.

Using strategic and organizational methods, leaders can effectively manage silos and avoid, or overcome, OM without resorting to the overly drastic measures which ultimately have no positive effect. There are several strategic and organizational methods (*shown in Table 1*) that, when applied will, over time, positively affect an organization and help it overcome OM. They are designed to provide targeted results for leadership and the organization as a whole.

Table 1: Strategic and Organizational Methods to Overcome OM		
METHOD	**RESULT**	**TARGET AUDIENCE**
▸ Training ▸ Education ▸ Mentoring ▸ Coaching	Leadership Development	Leadership Only
▸ Strategic Planning	Strategy and Vision	
▸ Performance Management	Accountability	
▸ Change Management ▸ Employee Engagement	Culture	Leadership and Employees
▸ Organizational Design	Reorganization and Governance	
▸ Process Management ▸ Process Improvement	Cross-functionality and Customer Focus	Employees Only
▸ Human Capital Strategy ▸ Financial Strategy	Resource Distribution	
▸ Strategic Communication	Communication	
▸ Information Technology	Integrated Operations	

These OM strategic and organizational methods have two audience groups--leadership and employees. We will examine how these two target audiences behave, when an organization is suffering from OM, to obtain an overview of the methods' impact on overcoming OM. Later, we will explore the application of each methods to each audience group to achieve desired results based on the OM diagnosis of a particular organization.

OM, which is clearly a solvable problem, is often exacerbated by leaders who fail to recognize and understand the symptoms present within their organization. If they do not recognize or understand the symptoms of OM, how will they realize there is a problem or, once realized, understand the nature of that problem? The leader becomes frustrated by the negative consequences of his or her organization's affliction with OM, but lacks a clear understanding of what is causing the OM within the organization and why.

Leaders are responsible for developing and implementing strategies, holding personnel accountable, driving changes in culture, and ultimately for their organization's success. Without effective leadership focused on implementation and management of the strategic and organizational methods outlined in Table 1, OM will take hold and not be overcome.

With or without the direction of leadership, the actions of non-leadership employees will drive cultural norms within an organization. Employees are a key component to organizational behavior and governance success because, as a group, they fit and work within the organizational structure.

Although leaders' decisions will influence operations, resources, communications, and information technology from a high level, it is the employees who actually make things happen.

While all organizations require effective operations, resources, communications, and information technology to operate effectively, dysfunction within one or all of these areas will cause OM to thrive. Thus, an organization must attain the proper synergy between leadership and employees, and neither group should be ignored when overcoming or avoiding OM. Essentially, overcoming OM requires a whole-systems approach to organizational change. Leaders must influence change through their activities and employees must respond to those leadership actions and change their day-to-day methods of operation based on the strategic and organizational methods shown in Table 1.

While employees are a much larger group to influence and change, effecting change in either leaders or employees is equally difficult. Leaders must evaluate the organization's effectiveness in the areas of operations, resources, communications, and information technology, and any additional area considered key to that organization. Leaders should identify symptoms of OM or problems within those areas, understand the nature of the problems, and address them to overcome root causes to combat OM.

As stated earlier, OM sets in slowly, over time, and it is easy for both employees and leaders to become so short-sighted they do not realize that they are part of the problem.

And, because the organization's culture forms over time to simply "be this way," OM is often not easily noticed, nor quickly overcome. Accordingly, overcoming OM requires a systematic application of a full-spectrum of strategic and organizational methods.

Section 2
Design and Layout of this Book

This part of the Introduction explains the design of this book. Most sections present examples of what happens in a typical organization through the characters' interaction in our fictitious agency, Myopia.org. These examples are designed to facilitate your identification of activities or problems within your organization and to know what to look for. Then, each section will suggest ways to overcome the problems described. The goal of this book is to give you the ability to diagnose OM, and to provide you with the tools to overcome OM and improve your organization.

Myopia.org is significantly afflicted with OM. Throughout this book we will explore the issues the agency is faced with because of OM. Below (*shown in Figure 1*) are the organizational departments and players in the agency that we will be following throughout this book.

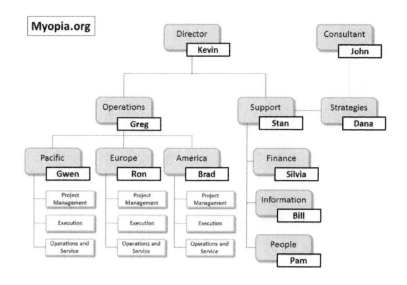

Figure 1: Myopia.org Organizational Structure

This book is designed not only as a story of Myopia.org's struggles, but as a guide and reference for you to use repeatedly. It is written in such a way that you can read the entire book as the story about Myopia.org unfolds in front of you.

However, from a technical and teaching perspective, this book provides you with the tools to improve any organization facing OM-related issues. As a reference, this book is designed to provide you with strategic and organizational methods that you can apply. Like a surgeon, you can identify specific OM-related symptoms within your organization and provide solutions to cut out the root causes.

Part One of this book is the Introduction you are now reading. Its goal is to provide you with an understanding of the subject and how the book is laid out. Part Two explains the concept of OM in greater detail. It provides expanded descriptions of OM, so it is a good idea to read Part Two next rather than skipping ahead in the book. Part Three discusses the two Strategic and Organizational Target Audiences (see Table 1)--leadership and employees--in greater depth. Part Four covers each of the Strategic and Organizational Methods (see Table 1) and how to employ them to fix specific Strategic and Organizational Target Audiences' issues. This part is also set up as a reference so that you can diagnose a specific problem area within your organization and identify surgical ways to deal with the problems and issues that you diagnose.

The organization we will examine as our case study for this book (see Figure 1) is a small operational agency which is part of a larger organization and goes by the name of "Myopia.org." The organization could be government, nonprofit, or commercial in nature, as its issues are consistent with any organization might also face. Myopia.org employs about 200 people and possesses a standalone function that serves a specific customer base by providing key products and services--the specifics around these products and services do not matter. As we proceed through this book, we will learn more about Myopia.org, its problems related to OM, and how it went about solving them.

The problems in these examples cumulatively model a completely dysfunctional organization, but can be reviewed and dealt with individually. Any reference to names or situations is purely coincidental, as this agency is not intended to represent any specific real-life organization. The situations portrayed in this book are typical to many you will find in your own organization, or in others. The intention is to make the case studies as real as possible, so you can identify with the situations and solutions in our fictitious agency and relate them to those that your organization might be facing.

Part 2

Organizational Myopia

Myopia comes from two Greek words: "myein," meaning shut, and "ops," meaning eye. Nearsightedness and myopia are also often referred to as "shortsightedness." As a myopic individual is shortsighted and not able to see things far away, myopic organizations are shortsighted and fail to see the big picture or do not have a long-term vision. This is called Organizational Myopia, or "OM."

The percentage of organizations suffering from OM is significantly higher than the percentage of people suffering from medical myopia.

Section 1
Impact of Organizational Myopia

Strategically, OM has a negative impact on organizations. Organizations that suffer from OM are reactive in nature, fail to focus on the same customer throughout the organization, and seldom have strong strategic planning activities. Let us begin by looking at several common issues you might encounter in an organization impacted by OM: a lack of communication; personal agendas; and a lack of end-customer focus.

Lack of Communication: When silos start to form, divisions, branches, and offices can stop communicating with each other. They look inward for solutions and refuse to share information with others outside the walls of their silo. They suffer from OM. And, all too often, OM causes these different parts of the organization to work against each other rather than work together. One section of the organization may pass work to another section without understanding what the other needs (or why) and, accordingly, receives work that never seems to be in the format it expects or requires. The sections also become competitive; thinking each are better than, or know more than, others, or thinking no one else does their work correctly.

Personal Agendas. Leaders in OM-impacted organizations tend to have the worst OM behaviors, compounding the problem. When they build walls and lose focus on what the entire organization is doing, they turn inward and focus only on their own issues. They look to grow their teams based on their desire to strive for a larger span of control that will lead to promotion or a bigger job.

Leaders strive for more manpower and money to feed additional work they have often created to justify their current position or even future promotions. This growth is normally at the expense of other divisions, branches, or offices across the organization. Often this empire-building related growth is financially detrimental to the organization as well as to its component parts.

The organization that fails to focus at a strategic level on what it needs to meet its mission or vision is the organization that is focusing on personal agendas rather than the organization's future. It is on a path to failure.

Lack of End-Customer Focus: In many organizations, especially those with a specific set of customers, most processes should be focused on delivering a product or service to the end-customer. Organizations suffering from OM tend to focus on different customers for each process, which makes it harder for those organizations to deliver what is important to their mission--the product or service to that end-customer. In some cases, divisions, branches, or offices within an organization may even see themselves as their own customer as they work through their part of the process. Basically, they end up taking care of their own needs rather than the needs of anyone outside their part of the process.

In the next two pages, we will examine a typical business process.

Our sample organization collects customer requirements through a project manager, who is connected to the customer through the sales department. As the organization builds a customer's requested item it must be evaluated by finance, legal, and quality control before it is completed and shipped to the customer by the shipping department.

Consider the following:

▸ Sales, focused on making its end of the month quota, promised the customer something it knows the organization cannot deliver

▸ The Project Manager, working on a deadline, knew he could not get the complete materials and specifications necessary for manufacturing to build the product, but submitted the order anyway to meet his required deadlines

▸ Manufacturing attempted to build the item to the specifications provided, but realized it could not fulfill the request without further information and research

▸ The project was delayed for months as Manufacturing worked through Sales and the Project Manager to get the specifications and create the right product

▸ When the item was finally developed, it was reviewed by Finance and Legal before shipping

▸ Finance refused to validate the price Sales quoted because it did not fit into its standard pricing model.

▸ Legal held up release of the product because it had experienced problems in the past with this customer and that made it uncomfortable with the risk of the sales relationship

▸ Quality Control rubber stamped the work, so the product passed without issue, even though it did not meet the customer's requirements

▸ The final product was finally released to Shipping; however, the delivery was delayed on the dock for a week because of other self-prioritized shipments

Few, if any, of these parts of our example focused on the actual end-customer. When the customer finally received the product produced and shipped, it was not what they expected, not received when they expected it, and cost more than the original quote by Sales.

As you can see, an organization suffering from OM is usually riddled with issues and problems. When OM exists, all parts of the organization do not operate successfully together, which prohibits the whole organization from operating effectively and efficiently. This also prevents it from seeing the big picture or long-term view.

Often, it is not apparent to members of the organization that it is suffering from OM. Leaders and employees are normally aware that something is not working the way it should. However, they do not know what the cause is. Many people working in an organization suffering from OM will be frustrated and might give up on trying to get things done right. And, unfortunately, when leaders realize their organization is suffering from issues because of silos, they frequently resort to drastic and ineffective solutions.

Section 2
Organizational Redesign as the Traditional Response

The traditional response from organizational leadership to the symptoms of a siloed organization suffering from OM is to redesign the organization or move people around. These actions usually fail to achieve the desired results and, often, create quite the opposite.

Leadership might realize there is a problem. They see the failures to communicate across departments. They witness people only looking out for themselves or their team. Evidence is apparent that the organization is not effectively or efficiently meeting customer needs. However, leadership does not know how to appropriately respond. They assume the problem is with the structure and personnel, and decide to "fix it" by shuffling the deck.

Moving people around within an organization or, worse, a total reorganization, is very disruptive to work centers and the employees within them. Relocated people must learn new processes, often requiring training that takes them away from productive work, and discontent can surface if employees misunderstand or disagree with the change. Remember, moving people around and corporate reorganizations require change, and it is human nature to resist change. Further, if this "fix" is one that leadership applies often, each "fix," or change, becomes harder for the organization and its employees to endure. Thus, effectiveness and efficiency will

31

continue to decline and these reorganization actions, by themselves, seldom work. They cannot help but fail to achieve the results leadership expects (or hopes for). Why? The actions fail to deal with the root cause of the problem-- OM.

As previously discussed, most organizations are naturally siloed. However, that does not mean they have to suffer from OM! The focus of this book is on overcoming OM, which does not necessarily require breaking down silos or totally discouraging a siloed structure. OM can only be overcome by learning to identify OM and its symptoms; by understanding what is going on within the organization; and by learning how to effectively work within silos.

Section 3
Root Cause of Organizational Myopia

What causes OM? People's innate need to belong leads to the formation of groups. Smaller groups within the larger organization tend to focus solely on the smaller group's needs. OM then starts to form because these groups begin to only look inward. Doing away with groups will not do away with OM because people and organizations need them.

This is the root cause of OM.

We have established that humans tend to form into groups. In fact, we are seldom psychologically effective if we do not have a social group to belong to. Think about some time when you were at work and had a problem with your personal life at home--you had trouble concentrating on work; you may have made mistakes; and your focus was else-where. We suffer from those same distractions and feelings when we lack strong social bonds or a group to belong to at work.

Reflect on the last time you started working with a new team, either moving to a new organization or changing teams within your existing organization. Your first few weeks, pos-sibly more, were awkward or uncomfortable as you got to know the people on your team and they got to know you. Your first few weeks or months in the new team were proba-bly filled with training and orientation. As you became more knowledgeable about your job, you started to build personal and working relationships, both within and outside of your team. These relationships became strongest within your own team. As these bonds grew stronger, you start to see the team as an effective group working well together on projects and your focus is mostly inward on your team.

When something goes wrong (and it almost always does), your natural defensive mechanism is to turn the blame on others outside the team, the group with which you most strongly identify. The tighter the group, the easier it is to shift the blame elsewhere. And often, individuals in these work groups can become very close. This is especially true with employees who have few connections outside the workplace.

You may recall a time when you have been in a close-knit employee group--you may be in one now. For many people in business, especially in non-leadership roles, the circle of influence of other employees becomes smaller and smaller. Think about the size of the group you are in, or were in last. That narrow sphere of influence promotes and causes OM.

At the leadership level, you might argue that the leaders must interface with other leaders within the organization regularly. To some degree, that is true. However, when leaders only interact with other leaders, it can sometimes cause employees and leaders to take an "us versus them" view. How many times have you heard something like, "They (employees) don't know what we know, so they can't understand the situation," or "They (leadership) sit up in their 'ivory tower' and don't understand what it's like on the floor?" These kinds of comments are indicative of an organization suffering from OM.

In most organizations, the leaders meet on a regular basis--normally weekly. These "staff" (or leadership) meetings generally consist of everyone reporting what they did last week and what is coming up in the following weeks. The meetings are used to disseminate information between leaders with the hope that such information will filter down to all employees. Sometimes, these kinds of meetings are used to embarrass leaders by openly reporting on meaningless measures of who did and did not get certain annual training done or who is late with performance reviews.

Regular staff meetings are necessary for everyone, leaders and employees, to stay abreast of what is going on in the organization and to maintain synergy. However, it is common for leaders to merely attend such meetings as representatives of their siloed section of the organization and not to further working together as an overall leadership team. In fact, in some cases, leaders might even be scheming about how to use the leadership meeting forum to gain more power in the organization for themselves (i.e., to build their own empire) and thus increase OM.

Keeping this in mind, consider how drastic reorganizations of an organization suffering from OM can do more harm than good. Employees will flounder around as they learn new skills, but more importantly, they will not be productive members of the organization until they have rebuilt their social networks and start to feel like they are part of a hardworking and successful team. In some cases, these employees will quit or refuse to work at all--especially if reorganization has become the regular tactic of the organization or its leadership.

For the most part, leaders experience the same issues related to OM as employees. They might experience a great deal of frustration or resentment because of their actual or apparent "loss of power." Months and years of hard work by an individual leader building, scheming, and plotting could be ruined in a single reorganization. This might result in the leader's immediate attempt to rebuild his or her empire back up to the status it held before the change. In some cases, these leaders might leave the organization. This might ultimately be desirable, but remember, the knowledge and experience goes with them too. Plus, replacing senior leadership can be a timely and expensive endeavor.

As you can see, attending to the basic physical and psychological needs of employees and leaders in any organization is important. Jeopardizing these needs can lead to fear, uncertainty, resentment, and anger, creating even more problems for the organization. This will ultimately lead to the re-formation, over time, of silos and the organization will eventually revert to its previous ways and methodology that existed before the organizational change. Worse yet, failure to attend to these physical and psychological needs will result in productivity losses and potential personnel losses that can do even more harm to the organization.

So, what have we learned? OM is caused by groups, formed naturally, who focus only inward for a variety of personal reasons. The key to effectively overcoming OM in an organization is to learn how to leverage strategy and organizational methods to work within the existing silos, deal with the root causes of the OM, and not react to its symptoms.

Organizational redesign and personnel relocation might be a part of the solution. However, that should only be undertaken with a solid understanding of the impact of such a change and an open-minded expectation of results.

Part 3
Target
Audiences

The sections within this Part discuss the two audiences who are affected by OM and who must be identified within your organization. Within every organization there are different types of people performing numerous roles. As is often and obviously stated, without people, an organization would not exist. People are an organization's greatest resource. But smart leaders see their people as more than "resources" or "human capital" even though they are often forced to use these terms to refer to the people that make up the organization.

We will focus on the two types of "human resources" in any organization--Leadership and Employees. These two parts of an organization's "human capital" are defined and described below. It is important to delineate between these two groups within the organization with respect to their involvement in, and the effect of, OM.

We will first review the leadership group, second the combined leadership and employee groups, and finally the employee group on its own. We break these groups out to allow you to understand the differences in how OM can affect each group and to focus your efforts on the relevant audience when looking for, and solving, OM-related problems. However, always keep in mind that in many organizations, the problems start at the top. Thus, fixing the deeper OM-related problems in the employee group without first focusing on the leadership group will prove to be less than effective.

Section 1
Leadership

The leadership group of an organization consists of the top-level and mid-level leaders and managers. These are the people who provide strategic, operational, and tactical direction to employees. Employees follow the leaders. They take direction from leaders. And, most importantly, employees emulate (both consciously and subconsciously) the traits and actions of their leaders. An organization that wishes to pattern a change (i.e., set the example to make a change successful), must first change through and by its leadership. If the leaders are doing something--anything--the employees see that as the measure by which everyone is held accountable.

This book is not meant to provide an education in effective leadership. Rather, it seeks to demonstrate the impact leaders have on an organization related to creating and overcoming OM. Even so, remember that any organization suffering from the symptoms of OM should first look at leadership when evaluating a proposed solution. Why? Because quite often, this is where the problems that lead to OM start. And, if the leaders do not believe in the solution, it will not work.

Truly effective leaders can self-analyze and determine personal areas for improvement. This book provides the standards, via examples and discussion, for leaders to conduct that self-analysis so they can modify their behavior, remedy certain issues within the organization, and overcome OM.

There are five key areas, listed below, in which leaders have an impact within their organization. Leaders should look for symptoms related to OM within these areas. And, to effectively rid an organization of OM, the organization should first diagnose and make necessary fixes to the leadership group related to these five areas. The top three areas fall solely within the leadership group, while the last two affects both the leadership and the employee groups. The top three relating to leadership should be evaluated and fixed (if issues exist) in the order presented. The five key areas are:

▸ Leadership Development
▸ Strategy and Vision
▸ Accountability
▸ Culture
▸ Reorganization and Governance

These five areas, as well as some that only affect employees, are discussed in Part Four of this book.

Section 2
Employees

The organization's employees are people who work for and follow the directions of leaders of the organization. Often referred to as "individual contributors," employees vary from the type of work they perform, the hours they work, how much they are paid (if they get paid), and how much control they exert within the organization through their jobs. The key difference between leaders and employees is that employees do not have the role of formally leading or managing others. Every organization has its share of informal leaders-- those to whom others look up and emulate, but these relationships are not categorized here.

Within the employee group, OM-related symptoms fall into six areas, listed below. The top two are the same as the bottom two symptoms seen in leadership. Unlike the top three leadership issues, the employee issues can be solved in any order, regardless of the order in which they appear in this book.

Take caution not to reorganize an organization without evaluating and correcting OM-related issues first. Many organizations jump right to reorganization when they start to experience OM symptoms, as reorganization is often seen as a panacea. Not only does it seldom fix the problem, as was discussed previously, it often makes it worse. Below, are the six employee group items we will explore in Part 4 of this book:

- ▶ Culture
- ▶ Reorganization and Governance
- ▶ Cross-functionality and Customer Focus
- ▶ Resource Distribution
- ▶ Communication
- ▶ Integrated Operations

Of course, the bottom four areas might impact leadership as well as employees, but we will address these problems with respect to the frontline employees.

Part 4

Overcoming Or-
ganizational
Myopia

Part 4 of this book is the "meat" of the material. Each section of this part covers specific methods to overcome typical symptoms occurring in an organization suffering from OM. The nine areas we will cover in Part 4 are:

1. Leadership Development
2. Strategy and Vision
3. Accountability
4. Culture
5. Reorganization and Governance
6. Cross-functionality and Customer Focus
7. Resource Distribution
8. Communication
9. Integrated Operations

At the beginning of each section, we will take a glimpse at life in Myopia.org to get an understanding of what is happening within the organization and how it suffers from OM. Much of the section will then discuss the symptoms organizations face when afflicted with OM and methods to overcome the causes. Finally, we close out the section by seeing how Myopia.org dealt with the causes of its OM.

The purpose of this book is not to teach you how to develop a leadership program or a strategic plan, or items in any of the other nine areas we will discuss. Rather, it is to explain these nine areas so that you can identify problem areas. Then you can address them to breakthrough silos and overcome OM within your organization.

Section 1
Providing Leadership Development

Kevin sits in his corner office and stares out the spacious windows that overlook the small lake and park near the organization's headquarters. Three years ago, he took over Myopia.org, replacing a twenty-year veteran of the company. As an outsider, Kevin's boss hoped Kevin would turn around several negative trends facing the company at that time.

During Kevin's first year, he learned what went on at Myopia.org on a day-to-day basis and saw many dysfunctional behaviors within the staff. About half way into that first year, Kevin started the search for someone with a background in strategy and management consulting. About two years ago, he found and hired Dana to lead a new Strategies Branch and he also decided it was time to reorganize Myopia.org to make it leaner and more focused on Operations.

First, Kevin took Stan off the Operations floor, put him over the Support Division, and gave him the direction to better align Support's missions to Operations' activities. What he was seeing, at the time, was that the Support Division was not focused on Myopia.org's primary purpose and it needed someone from Operations to better lead the team.

Next, Kevin reorganized Operations. There were two Operation Divisions--one focused on accounts in the Americas (North and South) and one focused overseas (Pacific and Europe). When the Division Chief of the Overseas Division decided to leave the company for a new job, Kevin merged the two divisions into a single Operations Division and put the Americas Division Chief, Greg, in charge of the newly consolidated group. He allowed Greg to organize the new division as he saw fit with the focus to improve efficiency and effectiveness.

Two years ago, Kevin thought his organizational changes and creation of the Strategies position would solve the problems Myopia.org was experiencing. However, things seemed to only get worse. Productivity declined further and he recently began hearing complaints from all over the organization.

Kevin's boss is now asking questions about employee and customer satisfaction and he's threatening to replace Kevin with a new Director. With his job in jeopardy, Kevin thinks desperately about where he went wrong and why the Myopia.org leadership team has not been more effective. Dana recently suggested he consider bringing in an outside consultant to discuss the issues he is having and ways to improve things. Maybe that would be a good idea.

Myopia.org's leadership problems are far from uncommon. As you read about Kevin's situation, you may see similarities to many organizations you have worked with or known in the past. Quite possibly, you work in this type of organization now or you might be a leader in a similar role or situation as our friends Kevin, Stan, or Greg--the Myopia.org Leadership Team. While it might be easy to focus on the things Kevin has done wrong, what is important is that Kevin cares about Myopia.org and its success. Kevin is trying to improve things, but his efforts have fallen short of solving the company's problems and he does not know why they did not work.

Later in this book, we will further explore Kevin's actions and their effect on the organization. Often, far-reaching problems in organizations, like Myopia.org, can be traced back to the leaders in charge and the actions they took or did not take. In extreme cases, leadership is poor or simply does not care. However, many leaders truly care about their job and their organization, but see that things are just not working out and they do not understand why.

Leadership is hard. There is no "playbook" to follow. Sure, there are courses to take and degrees you might seek, but the subject of leadership is broad and not always easy to grasp. OM begins to form when poor leadership exists--some researchers and authors refer to this as "toxic leadership." Most leaders do not recognize the gaps in their own leadership development. So, how do leaders overcome this knowledge gap to become effective at their jobs?

Through purposeful leadership development, which will enable them to better recognize OM and effectively start to overcome it.

Generally, leadership development involves developing the leadership abilities and attitudes of individuals within the organization. People are the most important resource an organization possesses, and smart organizations focus on the development of this important resource. Leadership development companies and consultants normally provide their services via a combination of continuous training, education, mentoring, and coaching of the organization's people.

How do you start? The first step to effective leadership development is accepting that there is a need for it. You might think you are a good leader, and you probably are (you are reading this book after all). But the fact is, the leaders in your organization need consistent external, as well as internal, guidance to continually improve and be their best. A week-long class for senior members on leadership is a good start, but that is not enough. Leadership development should be continuous.

Effective Leadership development is a deliberate and ongoing process. Key aspects of an effective leadership development program for any organization are:

▶ Consistent, constant, and delivered over time
▶ Tailored to overcome leadership deficiencies in the senior staff

▶ Focuses on the three main areas of leadership development:
  ○ Developing new leaders
  ○ Sustaining existing leaders
  ○ Preparing for leadership replacement

Consistent and Constant Leadership Development: Organizations that identify a need for leadership development often look for the quick leadership seminar to "check the box." They might send their leaders to an annual seminar or an event with a series of speeches from influential leaders and celebrities. Some organizations send members to a one- or two-week training program designed to craft better leaders, while others provide education and training opportunities in-house. These are all good efforts at leadership development, but a strong program requires a systematic combination of training, education, mentoring, and coaching.

Training consists of specific courses targeted to the individual and focused on increasing his or her leadership capability over time. It includes short- and long-duration leadership classes.

Education is obtained by attending seminars, hearing guest speakers at events, and reading and discussing leadership literature, including books, magazines, and blogs. Schools like Wharton provide excellent executive-level educational programs.

Mentoring requires matching a person with strong leadership abilities in a particular area to an individual leader who needs specific development in that area. The mentor provides guidance to the leader to help him or her improve. Mentors are often individuals within the organization. However, effective mentorship can also be found outside the organization.

Coaching normally involves bringing someone external in to advise, discuss, and guide leadership actions. Executive coaching, often seen as a luxury, ought to occur in all organizations. Having someone specifically tasked to help leaders identify their blind spots is crucial to development.

Having a broad leadership development program means consistently delivering all four of these areas to the organization's leaders.

Tailoring Leadership Development: Leadership development programs, like any education and training effort, are most effective if created based upon a needs assessment done with the group who will be utilizing the program. Since the program is focused on a small subset of the organization's personnel, it is easier and more effective to conduct focused assessments on individuals versus the group. Many consulting firms provide specialized individual assessments using tools like 360-degree and emotional intelligence assessments, as well as other tools focused on leadership motivation, style, and culture. These assessments identify potential challenges in a leader's capability that can then be addressed in more focused training, education, mentoring, and coaching.

Sometimes, an assessment might demonstrate how a leader's seemingly positive traits might be perceived poorly by an organization's culture. For instance, you might be a very confident and knowledgeable member of the staff with a take charge and get-it-done attitude. In some organizations this would be a very positive leadership trait. However, in a very collaborative environment, that same trait could easily be seen as arrogant and pushy by coworkers who are used to working as a team and discussing all options. Neither the trait nor the culture is wrong, but without realizing the potential conflict, misunderstandings can occur, and the organization ultimately suffers.

Targeted Leadership Development: For all positions within an organization there should be a solid plan of how to on-board new personnel, sustain existing personnel, and re-place personnel who have chosen, or are forced, to leave the organization. It is critical to have such a plan in place for leadership personnel. Additionally, organizations need a strong leadership development plan that targets leaders at all stages throughout the lifecycle of leadership--on-boarding, sustainment, and succession.

Organizations should also have a solid system of strategically determining who the future leaders of the organization will be so they can be prepared to replace someone who leaves or if the organization changes and requires new leadership. This should include a process of looking inside the organization and preparing future leaders, as well as vetting potential leaders from outside the organization.

By developing personnel internally, the organization effectively recognizes professional competence and growth. However, an organization that does not look outside itself for new leaders runs the risk of creating a stagnant pool of ideas and concepts. Bringing new leaders into an organization presents new ideas and concepts that can be key to an organization's future growth. However, it will do little to build loyalty within the staff and encourage personal development and growth. It is a balancing act.

Once an organization understands its needs for on-boarding, sustainment, and succession, leadership development programs can be developed for each of those areas. Targeting leadership development is nothing more than analyzing the gap between the current and desired state and determining how to close that gap through training, education, mentoring, and coaching. The key to targeted leadership development is to set a measurable standard and maintain that standard in a consistent fashion.

Strong leadership development should focus on a full spectrum of operational excellence activities. Traditional MBA programs generally only focus on financial management and accounting, marketing, and technology with a small amount of leadership and strategy. These programs often miss several important areas of executive education that include process improvement, change management, and employee engagement.

A strong leadership development program will include aspects of the following:

- Leadership and Management
- Strategy and Planning
- Leading Organizational Change
- Organizational Design
- Business Performance and Process Management
- Strategic Business Communication and Marketing
- Employee Satisfaction, Commitment, and Engagement
- Business Finance, Budgeting, and Strategic Cost Accounting
- Information Systems and Knowledge Management
- Business Process, Product, and Technology Innovation
- Business Globalization and Sustainability
- Fact-based Management (Theory, Research, and Data Analysis)

Developing New Leaders: To sustain an organization, you must sustain its leaders. A strong organization must have a good method for preparing new leaders to replace those that move up or move on. Succession planning, or talent-pool management, is a process of identification and development of internal people who have the potential to fill key leadership positions. Organizations well known for their succession planning and executive talent-pool management include: General Electric (GE)®; Honeywell®; International Business Machines (IBM)®; Marriott®; Microsoft®; Pepsi®; Boston Consulting Group®; and Proctor and Gamble®.

An effective succession planning program includes these key aspects:

‣ Identifies internal employees with the potential to assume greater responsibility within the organization

‣ Provides critical development opportunities and experiences to those who aspire to key leadership roles

‣ Ensures that all organizational leaders support the development of personnel through mentoring and guidance

‣ Links the organization's personnel database with a succession planning database to make better staffing decisions for key leadership opportunities

‣ Does not fear losing someone to a career broadening position when there is the possibility he or she might later come back to the organization with greater experience

An effective leadership development program can improve employee commitment and retention by meeting the career development expectations of employees. Also, preparing new leaders from within the organization can counteract the difficulty and cost of externally recruiting employees. But, remember that it is best to have diversity in leadership (in and outside the firm).

The first step to solving problems in a siloed organization is to ensure the leadership in that organization is able to identify and implement the required changes. As we have discussed, many times, the problems start with leadership.

A famous story goes that the founder of a 100-year-old consulting firm was fired by the leader of a company because the consultant told him he was "the problem" when asked to evaluate the company. It takes a strong and confident leader to honestly evaluate his or her own skills, capabilities, and shortfalls and then take action to do something to improve. It takes an even stronger leader to accept criticism from those around them. The 1837 Danish fairy tale, "The Emperor's New Clothes," is a perfect example of a leader out of touch with the reality around him.

By growing new leaders, sustaining existing leaders, and preparing for replacement leaders, an organization can begin to reduce issues that may be associated with silos and improve organizational operations. Without effective and knowledgeable leadership, regardless of any meaningful action taken, the organization will experience little sustained effectiveness.

Kevin, Dana, and the Myopia.org senior leadership team--Greg and Stan--met with John, a Management Consultant. They had discussed their leadership situation and issues and decided they needed some advice and guidance for the team. John and Dana worked together to develop a sustainable leadership development program that met the current and future needs of Myopia.org.

Together, they determined the needs of Myopia.org's three leadership categories (on-boarding, sustainment, and succession). They then developed a full-spectrum development approach for each category involving classroom training, continuing education, professional mentoring, and targeted coaching with John's consulting team.

Most importantly, Kevin allocated annual funds to the adopted leadership development program. The People department, working for Pam, was put in charge of implementing the program.

Every month, Kevin meets with John for an hour to discuss challenges, issues, and ideas. They have recently determined that the problems in Myopia.org run deeper than a need for leadership development. However, the leadership development actions they had taken were helping. They recognized that many of the solutions to the organization's problems were starting to become clearer to the leadership team as they developed their skills through targeted leadership development actions.

Section 2
Setting Strategy and Vision and Maintaining the Course

Dana, a recent MBA graduate, was very excited when she interviewed for the corporate strategy position with Myopia.org. Kevin, the CEO, hired Dana two years ago to help the organization improve through strategy and process improvement. She officially reports to Stan in the Support Division, but works directly for Kevin as her "strategic" boss. Myopia.org was facing several negative trends and a great deal of dysfunctional attitudes existed within the staff at the time she was hired.

Dana immediately set out to learn what Myopia.org did on a day-to-day basis. Within six months, she sat down and developed a mission, vision, and glossy strategic plan for Kevin to approve. Kevin was pleased and thought her product was perfect for the company. Myopia.org printed 200 copies of the strategic plan, which Kevin put into the hands of his superiors and shared with anyone who visited the organization--Dana even mailed a few out to key customers. They had distributed about half of the strategic plans over the last year or so. Two boxes of 50 each remain in the corner of Dana's office with a light layer of dust over them.

The initial excitement was followed by frustration about six months after the publishing and distribution of the strategic plan. The negative trends that hampered Myopia.org appeared to continue, if not get worse. Greg and Stan, the other

Myopia.org leaders, seemed to do everything but what was laid out in the strategic plan. And, when asked, most employees of Myopia.org did not even know the organization had a strategic plan, much less a mission and vision.

Kevin recently approached Dana with his frustrations and she recommended discussing the problem with John, their outside consultant, admitting that she might be in over her head. She didn't like admitting to Kevin that she was at a loss, but she realized that if something did not change soon, Kevin and Dana might be looking for other work.

This example illustrates the never-ending saga of strategic planning "shelfware"--strategic plans that are developed with good intentions and do little for an organization other than collect dust on shelves and coffee tables, or prop open office doors. Dana, like many people in her situation, started out with great goals and a lot of enthusiasm. Her approach to the situation was theoretically sound--start with the development and implementation of a business strategy. Organizationally, the working relationship she had between Greg and Stan was good--she had direct contact with and access to Kevin, the senior leader of the organization. So, what went wrong? Why did the strategic plan not seem to gain traction and help solve the problems existing in Myopia.org?

Too often, this tragic story plays out in businesses around the world. At least Myopia.org recognized the need for a business strategy; some organizations even fail in this regard. Myopia.org's problem was in oversimplification. Strategic planning is not simply the development of a strategic plan, because a strategic plan, no matter how well written, is not a magic pill that automatically improves an organization.

Setting an effective business strategy with a strong mission and vision and maintaining the course set out in that strategy is a systematic process and a culture change for many organizations. Most organizations that take the time to think strategically will apply some of the components, but few fully adopt a strategically cultural-mindset or apply strategic thinking. This is probably why approximately 70% of all strategic plans fail to improve the organizations for which the plans were designed.

Effective organizations follow a systematic strategic planning process. There are four phases of activity involved in strategic planning -- assessing, developing, implementing, and sustaining the strategic plan. These are defined as follows:

Assessing: Conduct all-encompassing and measurable organizational assessments annually, or on a similar recurring basis, to direct the organization's strategic plan development and facilitate the making of strategic decisions to grow and improve the organization.

Developing: Engage leadership, employees, customers, suppliers, stakeholders, and partners in the open review of organizational assessment results to develop strategies designed to reflect the purpose, direction, and needs of the organization.

Implementing: Develop step-by-step implementation plans using integrated planning teams with identified timelines and measures that provide accountability to strategic plan implementation.

Sustaining: Establish systems and processes to communicate, report, review, and guide the on-going strategic planning effort to ensure it is a "living process" and not just a one-time act.

Assessing: The first step to develop and implement a successful strategic plan in any organization is to properly conduct an initial, all-encompassing, and measurable organizational assessment. Every organization must take an honest look at itself to determine its core purpose (Mission), understand where it really is trying to go (Vision), and develop achievable objectives designed to strategically transition the organization from where it is now to where it wants to be (Goals).

Organizational assessments, especially the first assessment, can take several weeks to several months to complete. Factors that affect the assessment timeline are size of the organization, number of interviews, availability of staff, depth of research, and available time. For most organizations, this activity takes at least a month to accomplish. Once the organization establishes a repeatable method for assessing itself, future assessments can continue throughout the year, and annually, to feed recurring strategic planning activities. This builds to sustainability.

The Department of Defense (DOD) has a robust organizational framework designed to provide it with much of the needed information that feeds its effective organizational assessment. It calls the tool "DOTMLPF" (pronounced Dot-Mil-P-F). The DOD uses this joint military planning evaluation tool to measure the effectiveness of an organization's strategic or operational planning environment. DOTMLPF stands for Doctrine, Organization, Training, Materiel, Leadership, Personnel, and Facilities. Adding the additional components of

Financial, Relationships, Effectiveness, and Efficiency to this assessment (DOTMLPF-FREE) provides a deeper and more effective analysis for non-military organizations.

To fully appreciate how this tool works, we need to review the detailed components of the organizational assessment process of DOTMLPF-FREE, and identify how, and to whom, to present the results of this assessment. Hoshin Planning methods, which were developed by Japanese Professor Kaoru Ishikawa in the late 1950s, are also an effective way of assessing an organization but we will focus on DOTMLPF-FREE in this book.

The planning assessment process consists of two inputs: Primary and Secondary. Primary inputs are one-on-one interviews, focus groups, and survey assessment tools. Secondary inputs come from research in areas such as strategic alignment, organizational understanding, historical documentation, organization structure, manpower, funding, and existing measurement systems. It is important to identify all the secondary research materials that might be needed and start collecting them at the beginning of an organizational assessment. The information contained within these items is critical to the formulation of a general understanding of the organization and its issues to identify and develop interview questions that feed the primary inputs.

To ensure primary inputs are all-encompassing, interviews, focus groups, and survey tools should gain insight from a cross-section of leadership, employees, customers, suppliers, stakeholders, and partners. All primary inputs should be treated as confidential to protect anonymity in the process and generate true opinions. Remember that primary inputs are opinion-based. Thus, the information received should not be accepted as "fact," but rather recognized as "opinion."

The assessment should involve enough people to provide a valid representation, but does not need to involve everyone. Those conducting the assessment can determine an appropriate statistical sample size, if desired, but normally after about ten interviews, the same things tend to come up. By their nature, secondary inputs are more factual, but assessment observations developed from this secondary material are always biased by the assessor's opinion.

Together, the primary and secondary inputs provide a strong picture of what is going on in the organization. The results are usually documented in an assessment document of some type. From this material, the assessor can develop opinions that lead to a final evaluation and presentation. Be careful! As with observations developed from secondary material, opinions developed from only a couple of interviews, one subsection of the organization, or just a few documents are often flawed by bias. You will know you have enough information when you can validate the assessment opinions.

As stated, the DOTMLPF-FREE framework is a highly recommended approach to use to effectively obtain everything an organization needs to perform its self-assessment. Establishing a 1 to 5 scale scoring mechanism provides a repeatable process that can measure progress over time and can benchmark the assessment against other frameworks similar to DOTMLPF-FREE.

Below, the components of a DOTMLPF-FREE assessment are better described. The explanations are not all-encompassing, but merely a guide you can use to frame your own assessment.

Doctrine: The official military definition for doctrine from Joint Service publications is, "The concise expression of how military forces contribute to campaigns, major operations, battles, and engagements." Business doctrine is generally understood to mean, "The officially published and unofficially accepted directions that guide an organization." The doctrine of a particular organization can be identified through a review of several areas: existing strategic direction (i.e., plans, including things like mission, vision, values, priorities, goals, and objectives); company and business policies and directives; and procedural directions outlining processes, roles, and responsibilities (process documentation).

Organization: The organization component focuses not only on the organizational structure itself, but also includes the corporate governance systems. Corporate governance systems include things like the effective command and control (or span of control) within the organization, employee understanding of well-defined roles and responsibilities, as well as de-conflicted roles and responsibilities at all levels. An organization's structure also can dictate its internal communication effectiveness. Thus, communication applies here as well.

Training: To get a good understanding of the training component, determine if the organization has strong education, training, and professional development programs in place for its leadership and staff. Also, if this organization, as part of its role, is to provide training to others, how effective are its programs?

Materiel: Materiel looks at things like the organization's equipment, supplies, required machinery, communication systems, and information technology. Key things to determine are the age, effectiveness, and ability of these items. Also, from an information technology perspective, consider the overall integration of the information systems.

Personnel: The Personnel component is concerned with the full-time, part-time, contract, and outsourced labor of the organization. First, consider whether the organization has enough personnel. Then, determine if the personnel is aligned correctly within the organization and if it is the right type to perform the required missions. Also review whether the organization is getting the right return on investment from contract and outsourced assistance. Contract or outsourced assistance should only be used when it is cheaper; when the organization does not have the capacity or capability to perform the missions it is performing; or if the work is not long-term but is mission critical.

Facilities: Determine if the company has enough physical space to operate effectively, if it has too much or too little space, or if the space it has is being used efficiently. Examine the impact of geographic separations that affect employees' ability to work together effectively. If physical spaces are not neat, clean, and/or safe, this may impact the ability of the organization to successfully meet it mission's needs.

Financial: The Financial component includes analysis of the effectiveness of cost accounting systems and determines whether the organization accounts for the cost of quality and its return on investment. This component also examines whether the organization has sufficient current and long-term funding to be successful and resilient.

Relationships: The Relationships component is often overlooked. The assessment should focus on measuring the customers' opinion of the products and services delivered by each area. Also, the assessment should measure how effective the relationships with suppliers, partners, and collaborators are, as well as their opinion of the organization. Finally, this component examines the opinion of stakeholders outside the organization that do not fit into the above categories, but have a stake in what happens to or within the organization (e.g., shareholders, civilian communities, professional organizations, etc.).

Effectiveness: This component evaluates the process and operational effectiveness of each distinct product or service area within the organization. Measuring process maturity can be very handy here.

Efficiency: In this component, evaluate organizational and product and service area data by reviewing things such as activity-based costing, cost of quality, and return on investment to get an idea of organization's efficiency. Also, review processes to see how much value-added versus non-value-added work is involved.

Presenting the findings of the organizational assessment is a key piece of this first step and leads into the next step of the strategic planning process. When presenting the results of the assessment, provide the key points and recommendations up front and package the details at the back of the presentation or as a series of attachments. It is important to highlight that all the observations are based on findings from interviews conducted and research reviewed.

Keep in mind, this material should only provide information and recommendations, not solutions. The assessment should guide leaders in their development of the eventual solutions, which results in their "buy-in." The final assessment presentation, no matter what form, should have some important highlights:

Assessment Process: It is important to start the assessment report with a short discussion of the purpose of the assessment, the process used, and sources of input (primary and secondary) interviewed and researched.

Key Players: The key players section should identify the current organizational structure (emphasizing leadership) as well as customers, suppliers, stakeholders, and partners that interface with the organization. Key relationships should be identified first.

Mission and Vision Discussion: If the organization is subordinate to one or more organizations (as is Myopia.org in our example), show the strategic alignments of the mission, vision, priorities, goals, etc. of the various organizations, then focus on the observations surrounding the mission and vision of the organization you have assessed.

Other Assessment Results: There are many tools organizations can use to self-assess aside from DOTMLPF-FREE (e.g., Change Readiness Assessment, Culture Assessment, Stakeholder Assessment, Manpower Analysis, Process Maturity, etc.). If any other assessments were used, identify what tools were used and discuss the results from those tools.

Strengths, Weaknesses, Opportunities, and Threats (SWOT) Analysis: The SWOT Analysis is a high-level view of the Emerging Insights component (see below). It is normally framed into a quad chart for presentation and kept high level, but may be made more expansive if necessary.

Emerging Insights: As you conduct the assessment, certain themes or insights will start to appear. In military doctrine, these are called Emerging Insights. Use a Pareto Chart to prioritize the importance of these key observations to help leaders focus on the critical few versus the trivial many.

Developing: The second activity in the strategic planning process is to engage, as much as possible and feasible, a cross-section of leadership, employees, customers, suppliers, stakeholders, and partners in the development of the strategic plan. This will be the planning team. Although strategic planning is a leadership responsibility, involving others in the process helps to develop a fully-rounded plan. Leadership is also responsible for developing the mission, vision, values, core competencies, and goals of the organization.

Employees, customers, suppliers, stakeholders, and partners should be engaged during the process to provide input and comment on the development of these key strategic elements. Once the plan is developed down to the goal level, integrated employee teams, each led by a member of the leadership team, should take ownership of the plan and transition from the strategic to tactical levels of implementation.

Important to effective planning, in this second activity of development, is to openly and honestly present the details from the organizational assessment (the first activity) to everyone involved, using the presentation framework discussed above. The organization must learn to identify and own its problems. If an organization ignores major problems, everyone involved will realize the organization is not serious about fixing anything and people will lose interest in the planning process. Once everyone understands the organization's status at the time of the assessment, they can focus on developing the right essential strategic elements (mission, vision, values, core competencies, and goals) of the plan.

As mentioned, establishing mission, vision, values, core competencies, and goals is the expected result from this step in the process. Because leaders know they need to develop these things, they often end up creating a mission or vision statement that sounds good but is not future-focused nor is it effective at leading the organization to its future goals. Core values are often lofty and not realistic, and goals are generally created to represent the work of different parts of the organization rather than the needs of the organization as a whole. Thus, the rest of the strategic planning process is flawed, because leadership is just going through the motions of developing a plan.

Ways to construct effective mission, vision and values statements, and to create core competencies and goals are outlined below:

The Mission Statement: A mission statement should represent the core purpose of the organization. A simple quality technique that can be helpful when working towards identification of the core purpose (mission of an organization) is the "Five Whys." Often, an organization will write its mission statement to describes "how" it does what it does in a very program-specific fashion (it provides a laundry list of programs and functions it performs). This is ineffective because it limits the organization's understanding of "what" it actually does. Instead, the organization should focus on who it provides its products and services to--its customers--and ask, "Why do we do this and for what purpose?" Often, the simple act of asking "why" several times will lead to an understanding of the organization's core purpose.

Let us look at this example: A government civil engineering geospatial information system (GIS) entity listed its mission as, "Providing GIS systems and services to the customer." After better examining who it supported (i.e., military) and why it performed these functions (i.e., providing GIS systems and services), it redefined its core mission to, "Providing decision makers with geospatially-enabled data, tools, and materials to make better installation-related decisions." By focusing more on its customers and what they needed, the organization was better able to define what was important about what it was doing.

The Vision Statement: Once an organization better understands its core purpose (mission) and understands where it with respect to performing that mission (assessment), it can develop a vision statement that reflects where it truly wants to go. Too many times an organization states its vision is to be "world class" or "best in class" in its field, but it often has no idea what that means, how far it must go to get there, or even how to get there. Statements like those sound lofty and inspiring, but without substance, a vision statement becomes words without meaning--and everyone will know it.

A vision statement should be something that can be measured against and that people can actively work towards as well as forward reaching so that it drives behavior for many years. Otherwise, how wills the organization know if it achieved its vision? And, of course, the vision statement should inspire employees, while communicating to everyone outside the organization where it is heading.

Let us take a second look at our GIS example: Its vision was, "To be the world class provider of geospatial information services." This wasn't an accurate vision statement. GIS was the only organization providing this service to its specific set of customers. Further, it had no idea what it really meant to be a "world class" provider. When it reexamined its purpose and its current status, it was able to redefine its vision as: "Decision makers using effective and authoritative GIS data and tools." The new vision was not focused what the organization provided. Rather, it was focused on the expectations of it from its customers--decision makers. The shift was new, ensuring the customers were using the data and tools provided for effective decision making. This shift initiated a major success of the program.

Values: Values and core competencies (see below) are both very important to an organization, but each impact and influence an organization's strategy differently. Values, also referred to as principles, are the driving influence of how an organization operates. Values and core competences guide the mission and vision and the behaviors of personnel that work within the organization. If an organization has a problem with displayed behaviors, for instance a lack of teamwork and collaboration within the organization, a desirable value for the organization could be "teamwork." Normally, an organization's values are defined using one word. To avoid confusion among the organization's employees, broader values documents are published with expanded explanation and description of the values.

Core Competencies: Core competencies are as important as values (see above), but in a different way. Core competencies guide the organization's strategic planning decisions about what it does and how it does it. There are normally two ways an organization conducts strategic planning: inside-out or outside-in.

In inside-out strategic planning, the organization defines its strategic goals based on what it does (core competencies). This type of strategic planning is normally used by an established organization that already has a very specific understanding of what it does. (Military and service organizations traditionally perform inside-out strategic planning).

Outside-in planning is more often used in the commercial domain to find ways to grow market share or break into new markets. In outside-in planning, the organization determines the core competencies required to impact the desired market, then develops those competencies through its strategic efforts.

Regardless of which strategic planning method is used, core competencies must be identified in order to define what the organization will, and will not, strategically focus on doing. Similar to a mission statement, core competencies should not simply be a list of programs. Instead, the competencies should outline the core purposes of the organization as aligned to the mission.

Not all organizations develop values and core competencies because, although these are important tools, they are not always necessary. The results of the assessment will indicate whether the organization has a problem that will require the development of values or core competencies. However, when needed, they provide valuable information to organizations that effectively create and use them.

Goals: Setting goals is the first stage of developing an implementation plan, or roadmap, to enable the organization to meet its vision. Goals should be broad major milestones that will last as long as the vision remains valid. Objectives and initiatives are used to further define how the goals will be achieved. However, it is important not to get hung up on terminology (e.g., goals, objectives, and initiatives) when developing the structure of the strategic plan--we use these terms for the purposes of this book.

The completed strategic plan will have a broad layer of activities that outline the life of the vision (the goals), a more detailed layer covering several years (objectives), and a tactical layer of one- to two-year activities (initiatives). At all levels, the terms could be different, but the concept of "time" and "specificity" should always remain essentially the same. The best plans are created through brainstorming from the ground up (initiative-level), while focusing on solving problems, developing objectives through an affinity diagramming process, and developing goals through a tree diagramming process.

Implementing: Once the structure of the plan (mission, vision, values, core competencies, and goals) is created and agreed upon, the organization should develop a set of step-by-step plans. These plans should be implemented by integrated teams with identified timelines and measures that provide accountability for strategic plan execution. This level of action planning is a living process requiring constant review, refinement, and adjustment.

There are many ways to develop action plans at the initiative-level. However, it is important to remember that, at this level, action should be limited to the project, not program, level. For example, an initiative called "Execute "X" program," is programmatic in nature in that it never has an end. That makes it operational, not strategic. A strategic action should improve, create, develop, or optimize. In other words, these initiatives have a defined beginning and end. If your initiative takes several years, you probably defined it at too high of a level (i.e., objective). If the initiative only has simple actions, then perhaps you have defined it at too low of a level (i.e., action). Strategic planning is an art, but it is also an agile process requiring constant manipulation and review. Do not be discouraged if it takes you more than one attempt!

Sustaining: The last of the activities, sustainment, is the establishment of systems and processes to communicate, report, review, and guide the on-going strategic planning effort to ensure it is a "living process" and not just a one-time act. Having these systems and processes in place and active will help sustain your strategic planning effort. And, once you have these systematic components in place, properly resourcing and communicating your plan will be very important to its success.

Approximately 70% of all strategic plans fail to meet their desired results and about 30% of all strategic plans fail completely. By following the steps above to develop strategic planning, and by working at it, you can overcome these odds.

Seeking assistance from outside consultants can be helpful to an organization, but relying on the consultant to build the plan by himself or herself, is a waste of time and money. The plan must meet the needs of the organization. Consultants should only facilitate the development, not the creation, of the plan and present it as a finished product. An organization should be prepared to keep a consultant throughout the plan's implementation, unless it has dedicated staff prepared to drive the strategic planning process and sustain it into the future. Consultants can truly help an organization after initial plan development.

Organizations and employees need solid and inspiring direction that both makes sense and has sufficient committed resources to be effective. Strategic plans created in conference rooms by a few people and not guided by an honest organizational assessment or, plans that are improperly planned, resourced, communicated, and sustained, become nothing more than a pretty brochure that gathers dust on a coffee table.

When done right, strategic planning can be a very effective tool used to eliminate OM.

Given John's success working with Myopia.org on its leadership issues, Dana convinced Kevin to engage him in its strategic planning situation. John worked directly with Dana to review the assessment she had done when she started working with Myopia.org. Together, they conducted a robust organizational assessment involving leadership, employees, customers, stakeholders, and strategic partners. In a couple of months, they were able to present and discuss their findings with the organization's leadership.

Through facilitated meetings at the senior leadership level, Myopia.org redesigned its strategic plan, which everyone found to be much more responsive, effective, and inspiring than the previous version. Teams across the organization were formed to develop strategic objectives and initiatives, which were focused on improving the organization over the next five years. These plans were documented in project and performance monitoring systems, and everyone was given access to a strategic planning dashboard providing transparency to the entire plan, its status, and upcoming activities.

This was the first time Kevin really understood the direction his organization was moving.

Section 3
Providing Accountability Through the Use of SMART Metrics

Greg reviewed the operational measures one more time. Before him, strewn across his desk, were over 100 printed PowerPoint slides. Standing, for nearly an hour now, across from Greg, was a tall, slender man wearing a bowtie and small glasses that rested on his nose.

Brad ran the Americas branch of Myopia.org and one of his responsibilities was to consolidate the performance measures from the three branches: Americas, Europe, and Pacific. He fidgeted with the keys in his pocket, obviously nervous in front of his boss and shifted his weight from foot-to-foot trying to keep his legs from getting sore.

Finally, looking up from the many scribblings he had been making on the pages, Greg stated matter-of-factly, "I don't care how the operational measures are coming up, I'm not taking this data to Kevin. Make these changes and take out the slides I've marked. I've only got a month left here and I'm not going out with bad reports."

With that, he pushed the pile of papers across to the slender man, who quickly scooped them up. As Brad left Greg's office with the stack of annotated charts and graphs, he heard Greg's voice behind him, "I expect to see them on my desk in the morning."

Brad glowered at his administrative assistant as he passed her on his way into his office. She wisely kept quiet realizing that Brad's meeting with Greg went badly.

Brad tossed the pile of papers across his desk and slumped in his chair. He had worked all week putting together performance measures for Greg's program management review with Kevin, the Director. This was the first time in over two years anyone actually wanted to see anything aside from the profit and loss statements from the financial office.

Brad was rather excited that the new Myopia.org Strategic Plan was focusing on program-level metrics. Unfortunately, Kevin was not sure what measures were important, so he wanted to look at everything that was collected and, as a leadership team, review and determine what was important. So, Brad had very limited direction on what to put in his report.

The first problem for Brad was that Greg dragged his feet on Kevin's request, which Brad learned, came almost a month ago. Then, Greg gave Brad only a week to put together a presentation, probably because Kevin was making it an issue. Still, Brad was excited because many of the performance-measures they had tracked for the past few years were providing a very poor picture of the company's products, but Greg refused to do anything about it. Brad seriously thought action was finally going to be taken on problem areas and not brushed under the carpet.

Brad's attention turned to the carpet of his own office and he was tempted to pull up a corner of it and shove the whole set of slides under it. Instead, he logged onto his computer and set about the task of "making everything green" on the slides and, essentially, hiding all the problems Greg did not want to show. While the computer booted up, he called his wife and let her know he would be home late again.

Leadership not knowing what to measure in an organization and staff "adjusting" measures to make themselves look good are common problems within many organizations. You might be thinking to yourself that you have been in this very position before, whether you were in Kevin's, Greg's, or Brad's shoes.

So, how do these issues impact OM?

Understanding the performance measures that are important to the organization, aligning them to your strategic plan, and sharing them across the organization is one way to break down the barriers that exist in OM. If everyone is focused on different metrics and measures, or worse, no one is focused on measuring anything, the organization does not have a common understanding of what is strategically important and requires attention.

Some businesses attempt to adopt the popular balanced scorecard approach, which focuses the organization on key measures that transcend that organization's strategy. However, a good approach, this book is not designed to repeat this approach, but to discuss what performance measures are, what makes up good performance measures, and how to use performance measures as a strategic tool for your organization.

Performance Management Program

The best way to focus your efforts holistically is to develop a centralized performance management program within your organization that is aligned to your strategic initiatives. The program should be documented and managed through a performance management plan. The purpose of a plan of this type is to increase accountability among leadership and staff and improve overall performance of the organization.

Performance data highlights both effective and ineffective performance, guiding leaders to improve bad performance while sustaining high performance and achieving strategic goals. Aligned to an organization's strategic planning and process improvement efforts, the performance management plan outlines how sustainable performance measures will be collected, maintained, presented, used, and updated.

Additionally, as an annex to the plan, a performance measurement catalog is where all organizational measures should be maintained and tracked. This catalog is often maintained electronically so that is can be easily updated.

Collection and Maintenance. An organization's performance management plan should first address the measurement collection process. Normally, when an organization implements performance management, it already has some measures, although these measures may be poorly defined and tracked. The plan should highlight how to analyze the current measures, so leadership can identify opportunities for improvement and it should provide a process to recommend new measures to track performance. The main elements for each performance measure are listed below and discussed later.

▸ Measurement Details

▸ Method(s) of Collection
▸ Associated Timelines
▸ Range
▸ Standard
▸ Target

The performance management collection process should follow a simplified phased approach that is easy for employees to follow and easily repeatable. This process should be centrally controlled within the organization. The process should also tie into the organization's corporate governance. Typical phases are outlined below.

Phase 0: Identify a new performance measure. At Phase 0, an employee identifies a new potential performance measure. When the performance management approach is first implemented, several initial measures might already exist. As the organization moves forward with the performance management program, employees will identify new potential measures. The employees should sit down with the controlling agents to discuss the measures and the organization's governing body should determine if these are valuable to organizational decision making. If the measures are accepted by the organization, then each will be entered into the catalog and become better defined over time. Throughout the process, continue updating the measure's data elements in the catalog.

Phase 1: Define the performance measure. Once a new performance measure has been identified and accepted for collection, it should be aligned to the organization's strategic plan and a measurement owner should be identified by a planning team. Strategic alignment of performance measures ensures that the organization tracks how its performance strategically moves the organization towards its vision. If the measure does not support the strategy of the organization, ask why it is collected at all.

In this phase, a specific and concise name should be assigned to the performance measure. The name should be kept short and constructed in a manner that allows for future affinity grouping. The first word(s) in the measure's name should relate to the "thing" the measure is measuring (e.g., *personnel*). The last word(s) in the name should be what the measure is designed to assess (e.g., *turnover*).

By keeping the measurement name specific and concise, the organization can group similar measures together. In our above example, the measures catalog can be sorted by what is measured (e.g., personnel.) Sorting in this fashion will bring up all related measures and allow you to understand everything that is measured in relation to a particular subject. Thus, something as simple as effectively naming measures is important.

Also, in Phase 1, the owner should provide a full definition of the performance measure. At a minimum, the definition should include what is specifically being measured as well as the outcome expected from the collection of this measurement's data. At this point in the development of the measurement, it is important to refrain from directing how to collect the data or what the attributes of the measurement are.

Just concentrate on what you desire from this performance measure and focus on what decisions this measure will help leadership make. The following should be considered when defining a measure. The measure should:

▶ Be tangible--it can be measured
▶ Be testable--it should not lead to false assumptions of the process
▶ Be comparable--when looking at other like measures one can draw comparisons
▶ Be economic--it does not cost a great deal of money to collect and report
▶ Be based on regular, consistent, and identical collection
▶ Be limited to information that relates directly to the objective and goal and tracks progress toward achieving that objective and goal
▶ Produce timely, relevant, and concise information
▶ Provide results that compare to a program's intended purpose
▶ Provide information on the effectiveness of the activity or operation as it contributes to the goal or objective
▶ Lead to continuous process improvement and decision making
▶ Help describe organizational performance, direction, and accomplishments

Phase 2: Establish measure timelines. The first step in Phase 2 is for the owner of the measure to determine a proposed date to begin collecting data related to this measure. As a rule, an organization should only use data for decision making after the organization has enough data points to make an educated decision.

The owner of the measurement decides at what interval the data will be collected (e.g., daily, weekly, monthly, quarterly, annually, etc.) and from that can set a date when the data is mature enough to use for decisions. Some performance measures might have potential roadblocks associated with the collection of the data. You should determine what potential roadblocks might exist and develop alternative actions to mitigate these roadblocks before collecting the actual data.

Phase 3: Collect performance data. After setting the timelines for the performance measurement collection, the owner determines what method will be used to collect and present the actual data before the data is actually collected. This helps determine if systems need to be created to support this data collection effort and can lead to a better understanding of the data itself.

If a system for collecting the measurement data already exists then, obviously, it is best to use the existing system. If a system does not exist, a new method will need to be developed and implemented. It should be the focus of the performance management plan to consolidate as many data collection methods as possible for ease of use in data collection and presentation through an eventual dashboard.

Examples of data collection methods are a database, spreadsheet, data report, or possibly a specific software program. Be careful not to pull performance measures from an existing report that was designed to answer a different question without first validating the data behind the report. In the case of specific software or a system that collects and/or reports data, it is important that the performance measurement catalog have enough information about that system for incorporation into an eventual performance dashboard presentation method.

Once the method of data collection is determined, identify the specific location of the stored data. The location will vary by system, but the goal of the plan should be to consolidate as much of the data in as few locations as possible. Using something like cloud-based storage solutions, SharePoint®, or a shared drive can be very effective, but are not always the right choice. These methods are akin to creating a data warehouse of sorts.

The next step is to determine the appropriate data presentation method to enable effective decision making. Various presentation (charting) methods exist (e.g., pie chart, histogram, bar chart, line graph, scatter plot, box plot, etc.). Understanding how the data will eventually be presented will help when building a dashboard presentation method (see Must Understand Charts for Continuous Improvement). Once data collection begins, update the proposed data collection date to "actual."

Phase 4: Establish performance measure attributes. Without actual collected data, it is hard to establish significant attributes around the data. However, when the data reaches maturity, the owner of the data will recommend measure attributes (i.e., ranges, standards, and goals or targets) for discussion and approval (*shown in Figure 2*). Then, the data should be presented to corporate governance for review.

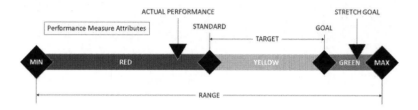

Figure 2: Performance Measure Attributes

Measurement Range. This is the range the measurement will take. Many measures use a 0 to 100 scale. Survey measures have data such as 1 to 5 or 1 to 7. Time is measured in days, hours, minutes, and seconds. The measurement range is the full range that is expected from the data, between the minimum (min) and maximum (max) possible data points.

Measurement Standard. The measurement standard is the level at which the organization should be performing. If performance falls outside of this point, the measurement (and hence the organization) is failing to meet the basic standards for that measure. Anything outside of the measurement standard is considered "red" (i.e., bad).

Measurement Target. As previously noted, "red" means that the performance does not meet standard. However, there is an acceptable range (yellow or amber) in every measurement, where the process is not failing, but could use possible improvement.

Measurement Goal. There is an established goal where the process is performing well (green).

Measurement Stretch Goal. Somewhere along the full range of the data, the organization sets a measurement point that it is working to achieve--normally this is a stretch goal.

All these attributes are created based on how the actual data is performing, what is expected by the customer, and what the organization can fiscally afford.

Presentation. The performance management plan should also define and describe the presentation approach to be used for the performance measures that are being collected.

Initially, it might be best to develop a manual (non-automated) approach to the collection and presentation of the measurement data to leadership. The organization should be able to institute this manual approach quickly and continue its use as a more-automated solution is developed for presenting measures (e.g., performance dashboard or technology system). The manual approach and eventual dashboard should link progress toward the organization's strategic plan and the health of the organization by aligning key performance measures.

Collecting and reporting measurement data can become a manpower-intensive job, so it is best to look quickly for automated solutions of the manual process and plan for this when developing the performance management program.

Application and Use. The data collected is only effective when used in a systematic manner to affect positive and continuous improvement (i.e., drive fact-based decisions). There are some key considerations to keep in mind when reviewing performance measurement data for your organization.

▸ Ensure you have enough data to make data-based decisions--at least six solid data points is best
▸ Use your data to set attributes and detect and correct problems related to those attributes
▸ Gain insight into, and make judgments about, the effectiveness and efficiency of programs, processes, and people
▸ Determine whether the organization is meeting the mission and moving toward its strategic goals and vision

It is important that the organization does not put too much faith in performance measurement data at its face-value. If performance objectives are not being met, it is obvious that something is wrong, but performance information itself does not provide the reason. Instead, it raises a flag indicating investigation is required. It is dangerous when performance objectives become numerical quotas and the quotas do nothing to drive improvements in the process. The alternative is to identify the challenges and make needed changes to the processes to improve performance and achieve the desired outcomes.

Performance measures provide a valuable tool for management and continuous improvement. However, people might try to "game" the system in a way that will make themselves and their programs look good, so be aware that the "measured system" is not always the same as the "actual system."

Performance measures also help form the basis for sound performance-based management, but the measures do not provide information on adherence to laws and regulations or the effectiveness of internal controls. Regulatory compliance requires other auditable materials to prove that things are occurring as expected.

The right performance data can lead an organization towards improving in a data-driven manner. The key is to not rely on the performance data as the improvement tool. Measurement data, when used correctly, is an indicator to potential problems in the organization and can help leadership invest crucial resources toward fixing problems and not tampering with processes. Below, are things to consider when analyzing performance measurement data.

▸ Ensure you have effective standards and targets for your measures and that the standards and targets are

not over-inflated and impossible to achieve--
measures should be specific, measurable, attainable,
realistic, and timely (SMART)

▶ Look at all measures for a holistic representation of
the organization and not just the few that are important at the time--using the strategic plan is a holistic approach

▶ When considering potential improvement areas, balance performance with cost of improvement, difficulty of improvement, and overall impact to the cus-
tomer--it is not always the worst measure that has the
most impact when improved

▶ Once you decide to look deeper into a performance
measure, ensure a strong quality approach is used to
determine root cause before making any adjustments

▶ If one data point drops, do not react immediately--re-
search the reasons and then wait for another data
point to move in the similar direction before striking
out on improvement actions (i.e., avoid "knee-jerk"
reactions)

▶ The best approach to continuous process improvements is a data-driven approach working in concert
with strategic planning and process management

Sustainment. The data captured through performance
management is only as effective as the currency of the data.
Assigning the management of the overall measurement program and ownership of each measure provides sustainability
of the performance measurement program. Once a new performance measure is identified, the program manager should

immediately begin updating the catalog and tracking the progress of the new measure's development. By remaining focused on new measure development, the process will not stall.

Every quarter, measures should be reviewed to ensure the data collected in relation to each measure is kept current and all attributes are up-to-date. It is helpful to conduct a review of one third of the measures each month to balance the workload over the quarter.

Once a year, in line with the annual strategic planning process, owners should validate performance measures to ensure the measures are still key to the organization being able to meet its goals and vision. Even though a strategic objective in the organization's strategic plan is no longer required, the performance measures associated with that objective may still be useful for the organization's success. Continue to track and measure data if it is important to the organization's operation and remove the measure only if it is no longer an important factor. This way, should the measurement start to falter, possible strategic initiatives can be redeveloped to target that area.

Performance Measurement in Silos

The above outline of establishing a centralized performance management plan and program, which is reviewed by the governance structure in the organization, significantly disrupts silos in organizations--silos that few people will even see. Often different parts of the organization measure things that are important to their operation, but that have little impact on the overall effectiveness of the organization in meeting its mission. When this happens, different parts of the organization end up competing with themselves without even realizing it.

A large cruise line found itself in this situation. It was noted by several guests that the pool temperature in the ship's pools were too cold for passengers to swim in. When this was mentioned to the staff, the issue was thrown over the fence to the engineering department, who maintained the temperature of all the pools. Engineering responded that everything was working, and the pools were being maintained at 80.6 degrees Fahrenheit temperature, which was set by the corporate office to keep the energy cost on the ships low.

Here, Engineering focused on measuring the bottom line cost of energy on the ship, while Hospitality was concerned about customer satisfaction. These two departments are on every ship in this cruise line and were at odds over their own performance measurements. The result was that the pools on the cruise ships went mostly empty for months, which was a waste of space and effort to heat at all. As well, this action developed a great deal of complaints from passengers because the pools were too cold to get in and enjoy, which was what the customer was essentially paying for.

By having Engineering and Hospitality identify their performance measures and align them to the strategy, leadership could evaluate these two measures--Energy Cost and

Customer Satisfaction--and determine what the appropriate tradeoffs would be for the cruise line to be ultimately successful. Until this happened, each cruise ship possessed an internal struggle caused by these important measures.

Traditional Measurement Approaches Do Not Change a Culture.

If you are a student of business, then you have probably heard all the quotes around measuring what you do. The bottom line is, if you are not measuring what you are doing, you cannot manage and improve it. Some organizations do not measure anything, others measure very little, and most measure stuff at too high of a level to do anything with the measures. So, the first step to creating a culture of continuous improvement and breaking through silos is to start measuring what you do at a level that drives decision making.

How many things do you need to measure to tell you how you are doing in business? Some organizations measure everything and anything. Many times, what is being measured is not something the business can do anything about. In some cases, the measures collected, reported, and reviewed, mean little to nothing to the operation and quality of the business. All too often, when things are being measured, what is being measured does not drive any change in behavior.

To run a quality organization, you only need to measure three things. These three simple measures are some that many organizations fail to collect, or if they do, they collect them at the wrong level and frequency. All too often, managers and leaders are focused at high-level aggregate numbers and measures with little understanding of what generates the data and what the impact is if the numbers go up or go down.

> **The key to measuring is to:**
> **measure it where the work is done,**
> **on every process,**
> **and every day.**

So, what are these three magical measures? The three things that you need to measure are:

1. How much work you are doing (Workload Volume).
2. How long it takes to do it every time (Process Cycle Time).
3. How well you do it every time (Process Defects).

If you measure each and every one of your processes on a daily basis against these three measures, then you can build a quality organization and a continuous improvement culture that helps eliminate issues related with the silos we always experience. People at all levels--employees, managers, and leaders--will not only know what is happening, but they will know why and where to focus their energy to fix and improve things.

Workload Volume--how much work you are doing. As said, you need to collect data based on every time you perform a process. This means that you need to have a way to measure every instance of every process. More than likely, you have some type of system that measures work coming in or going out of your organization. There is probably some sort of system of record that is quantifying the volume and type of work occurring within your organization. Take a hard look at the systems associated with your processes today and see what instances the system is counting. If you do not have any way to track the workload on a daily basis, then you need to build a system to do so.

It is important to collect work volume daily so that you can look at the process by individual days. Typically, especially in a service environment, work flows at different volumes between Monday and Friday. Medical, manufacturing, and the like normally include work flow seven days a week. It is important in any organization to look at work from a work-day perspective. Aggregating work volume to the monthly, quarterly, and annual levels is fine for management and leadership, but does nothing for managing the work where the work is done.

Once you have the data, put it into one system of record--a simple Excel spreadsheet will initially work, but other more advanced systems can be built or bought. When working with Excel, start with a data sheet showing the daily volume of all your processes for a specific team or group. From a reporting perspective, you can create three views: Annual, Monthly (January through December), and Workday (Monday through Friday, and Saturday/Sunday, if you process work those days). For each of these views, which could be tabs on a spreadsheet, you should look at your data in at least three ways:

1. Pareto Chart: the first view is a Pareto Chart of the total volume of each of your processes presented in that view (year, month, day). This will show you what processes are taking up the most of your time, and which are taking up the least.
2. Box Plot: the second view is a Box Plot of the total volumes from each of your processes presented in that view. This will show you the variance of volume of each process and the outliers of the volume.
3. Control Chart: the last view is an individual Control Chart of the volume of each of the processes presented in that view. If the view is for the year, then chart the data aggregated monthly. If the view is for the month, then chart the data aggregated daily. If the view is for a specific day (e.g., Tuesday), then chart the data for every work item of that day (i.e., the actual count. This will show the actual variance of the data between charted points.

Having this data collected and reported in this manner provides a powerful view into what is going on in the processes of the organization. However, by itself, volume is a statistic that really has little value other than providing a way to forecast potential future volume.

It is surprising to learn that, often, organizations do not have a view into their workload at this level. Build this type of view into your daily work, teach your employees how to read these three basic charts, and show managers how to predict their workload. If you see that Wednesdays and

Thursdays are always your lowest volume days, you now have a powerful planning tool for when to send people to training, when you can cross-train employees, when to hold that monthly team building event, etc.

Process Cycle Time--How long it takes to do your work every time. As said above, workload volume information alone will not tell you enough about your process to make data-driven decisions. Also, workload is not something you normally can control, especially if your processes are the result of someone else's process within your organization. This is often true of big companies with large end-to-end processes and value chains.

However, when you add in the second measurement item--time--you have a very valuable combination. Be aware, though, that measuring process cycle time can be a bit more challenging than measuring workload volume.

Some organizations have systems that automate and track the workload and processing time of what is done. These systems can take many forms, from home-grown to off-the-shelf. A couple of typical workflow automation systems found in organizations are Microsoft's InfoPath® or Salesforce®. If you have your processes on some type of automation like this, then harvesting the time might be relatively easy. That is, of course, if the systems were set up to track the process step-by-step and end-to-end. The most basic measures from the system are the start and stop time of the process, but if the steps are broken down in detail, you can get additional data. To start, you just need the beginning and ending times of the process.

In the absence of these kinds of automated systems, you need to measure the process cycle time in its current form. Every time you make process changes, you need to re-measure the processes cycle time. Doing this can be a bit time consuming, but is crucial to your operation's quality.

Outside of pulling process time from systems, there are two basic ways of measuring time: 1) good operator estimates and 2) physical timings. From an industrial engineering perspective, there are several other ways of timing a process, but these work best for most organizations.

Good Operator Estimates. This type of timing is what is often refer to as Weighted Per Accomplishment Time (WPAT). It is a pretty simple approach to get to an 80% answer for your timings. It also is easy to collect, which reduces the time and hours required--hence, it costs less to collect. Your timings are based on the personal estimates of people who work on the process and who are good at it. You do not want to interview people who are new or not very good and you do not want to interview your star employees, otherwise your estimates will be skewed. Try to interview or survey up to five employees who perform the process and then average the results. Here is how you do this:

▸ Step One. Select at least one, and up to five, employees who work in the process focusing on those who are good at the work. Base the number of employees you select on the number of employees who perform the function to obtain a good ratio.

▸ Step Two. Ask each of the employees three things: 1) How long does the process take on average (Average Time), 2) How long does the process take in the worst situations (Pessimistic Time), and 3) What is the fastest time that the process can be completed (Optimistic Time)?

▸ Step Three. If not already done, turn all timings into seconds. Seconds are the easiest to work with when analyzing and provide the cleanest view of the process.

▸ Step Four. Ask each of the employees two more questions: 1) Out of 100% of the time, how often does the Pessimistic Time happen, and 2) Out of 100% of the time, how often does the Optimistic Time happen? The remaining percentage (100% minus Pessimistic minus Optimistic) is the average (Average Time) occurrence.

▸ Step Five. Multiply each time (Average, Pessimistic, and Optimistic) against each of the corresponding percentages. This will give you three fractional times. Then add these three times together. This will give you a WPAT in seconds.

▸ Step Six. Average all the WPATs you collected from the employees to come up with a final Average WPAT in seconds. This is the estimated average that the process will take per instance it is accomplished.

If you perform the process an average of 100 times in a day, you can multiply 100 against the WPAT and you have a good estimate of how much total time is required to do all the work for the day. Multiply that number by the days that you work, and you have a good estimate of how much total time is required to do all the work for the year.

Some additional information can be gleaned from these timing estimates. If you look at the Pessimistic and Optimistic times, there is a range (Range equals Optimistic minus Pessimistic). This range reflects a variance in the process. If this variance is wide, or if the Pessimistic or Optimistic Time is way off from the Average time, you should determine why is there so much variance and what is happening. Perhaps you are really looking at more than one process or there are some serious exceptions in the process that could be ripe for process improvement. Additionally, if the estimated times per employee are significantly different, you should determine why the times are so different. Clearly at least one person is doing something different than the others and this can help you identify opportunities for improvement. Many times, this is due to lack of standard work.

Physical Timing. Physical timing obviously takes more time and effort and essentially costs more to accomplish, but it definitely provides a more accurate assessment of the process cycle time. It can be rather time consuming to have only one person conduct the timing effort. Rather, you can establish a formal and documented timing methodology and turn this methodology over to the process owner to own the timing. This way, the owners feel more comfortable with the result and can re-time the process following the documented steps every time the process changes. All you have to do is analyze the data when they are done. Below, are the steps to conduct this style of timing:

▶ Step One. Establish a specific person who will conduct all the timings for the process. They must understand and follow the process. Otherwise the timings could be collected incorrectly. The same person should collect all the timings for one process. Having more than one process timer on a single process, can cause confusion and you could end up with different timings for the same process.

▶ Step Two. Identify the process start and stop time by observing the process. It is important to start and stop the process at the same time for every timing to ensure accuracy.

▶ Step Three. Determine the number of process operators you will time. If the process is performed by one person, then obviously, you can only time one person. If the process is performed by less than 10 people, time 2 processors. If the process is performed by 11 to 25 people, time 3 processors. If the process is performed by more than 25 people, select 4 people to time. Try to ensure you select good operators (not new, star employees, or poor employees). You are trying to get a "good operator" average.

▶ Step Four. Outline a timing schedule based on the process. You need to determine what is the appropriate timing approach based on when and how the process occurs. For a normal process, which is performed constantly through the work day, Monday through Friday, consider this recommended approach. For each process operator, at 9, 10, and 11 a.m. take three timings. After lunch, at 1, 2, and 3 p.m., take three timings again. Try to take each timing back-to-back. This equates to 18 timings a day. Follow this approach for 1 week, which would result in 90 timings per process operator for the week. This is more than enough data to understand the process. You can double the number of weeks for 180 timings per process operator if you want. If the process occurs less frequently, or only on certain days, adjust accordingly, but try to obtain at least 90 timings per process operator with your approach. Caution: Avoid only collecting on certain days or at certain times, unless the process warrants this approach. For analysis, it is important to get a good picture of the process throughout the entire work week.

▸ Step Five. Conduct the timing following the schedule developed above. Use this schedule if the process changes to re-time the process. Time everything--do not throw out timings or stop because of exceptions in the process. If something happens during the process that causes it to take abnormally long (e.g., process exceptions, taking a phone call, having to get supplies, answering a question, etc.) write down what happened during that timing that was unusual. This is important data at this point as these situations are currently part of the process.

▸ Step Six. If not already done, turn all timings into seconds. Seconds are the easiest to work with when analyzing and provide the cleanest view of the process.

▸ Step Seven. Now comes the time to analyze the data. The first thing you want is the average time. Again, do not throw out any of the data at this point--simply compute the average process cycle time by adding all the timings together and dividing by the number of timings. This is not the cleanest data at this point, but it is true data.

While this is the best process cycle time you can collect, it is just the start of the analysis...you can look at the quickest and longest times and obtain a variance, you can examine the variances, you can examine multiple process operators, etc. With this basic data, you can gather a great deal of information about each and every process you perform.

When you multiply volume of work and the time it takes, you obtain the total time it takes, by day, to perform the process. There are traditionally 2,080 available work hours in a year, which means there are approximately 173 hours available per month per person (2080 divided by 12). Combining available hours and required process time (Volume multiplied by Cycle Time), you determine how many full-time employees it takes to perform the work if they work 100% of their available time on the process. By knowing this, you can forecast required manpower by the day of the week and can prepare your operation for known surges in work. Suddenly, you have very powerful data for your operation!

Additionally, like volume above, you should look at this data using the same tools--Pareto Chart, Box Plot, and Control Chart.

Process Defects--How well you do the work every time. Knowing the work volume and process cycle time is very powerful information, but getting to a level of defect analysis really starts to help you manage and improve the process on a continual basis. Based on what you now know --Volume and Time--identify the processes that you want to examine first (i.e., those that have the highest volumes and highest processing times (use the Pareto analysis)). Do the following things to better understand the process:

- ▸ Map the process
- ▸ Observe the process
- ▸ Determine what exceptions exist in the process that cause variance
- ▸ Identify what does and does not provide value in the process

If you find exceptions in the process, these are probably actually "defects" in the process or an upstream process. Many times, people that work the process day-in and day-out do not see these items as "defects," but just "part of the process." Start collecting the number of times each exception occurs per day and, if possible, when the exceptions occur during the day. Use a simple check sheet to collect this data.

Analyze the results with a Pareto analysis to determine which exception you want to examine first. Look for ways to eliminate the defect and then move to the next one. To ensure the exception/defect does not appear again, never stop measuring for the defect.

Look for any waste when you do your analysis. Then look for ways to remove it or transition it to other less costly areas. Try to get your process to 100% customer value-added work.

This level of measurement work is seldom done in business--especially those of a service nature but is really quite easy to accomplish. Follow the three items and the steps and you will be on the road to having a culture of continuous improvement.

Must Understand Charts for Continuous Improvement

Unless you are in the business of process improvement or you live for statistics, you probably do not work with charts very much. However, to build a continuous improvement culture, everyone in your organization should have a general knowledge of some specific charts. They should know how to read and analyze them to make decisions.

The first thing to understand is that all charts are built from two basic charts that you see all the time--bar charts (also called column charts) and line charts (also called time-series or run charts). Understanding how to read and analyze these two charts is important, as these are the basis for many other important charts.

A bar or column chart is used for showing amounts in relations to each other (*shown in Figure 3*). These can be horizontal or vertical. Vertical bar charts are the more common presentation approach. These charts compare different areas or time frames with counts for each category and make it easy for the viewer to understand what is going on.

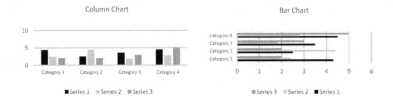

Figure 3: Column/Bar Chart

The line chart presents information plotted over a series with various dots, but the dots are connected by a line showing the continuous nature of the data (*shown in Figure 4*). An example of this would be monthly sales for the entire year.

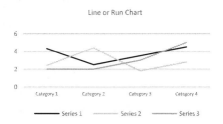

Figure 4: Line/Run Chart

In many cases bar and line charts can be used interchangeably and pretty much present the same data just in a different view. Understanding the basic charts helps you better understand the various other charts that are used to present more in-depth data for specific analysis.

Histogram. Uses a bar chart to look at values, or groups of values, over their distribution. With a histogram chart, you can look for the predictability of data in the process (*shown in Figure 5*). For instance, you can plot hourly volume for a process over an entire day if you look at in groups. This chart examines the distribution of the data under examination.

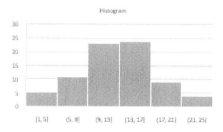

Figure 5: Histogram

Combining column and line charts in a skewed histogram view helps employees understand and use a Pareto analysis. Setting control and specification limits on line charts creates Control Charts. These are important charting tools that all employees should understand and are fairly simple to learn and use.

In summary, centralized performance management pro-grams, written out and managed using a performance meas-urement plan, helps an organization strategically manage and improve its operation. Organizations must ensure measures do not conflict and create silos within themselves. It is important to measure the key items of volume, time, and defects to promote continuous improvement.

Clearly understood measurement activities performed across the organization will go a long way to overcoming OM in a siloed organization.

As part of Myopia.org's strategic plan, Dana was able to establish the implementation of a performance management program using the advice of her strategic advisor, John. The first step was to review everything the organization currently measured. The leadership team found this lacking. Those measures that were already being collected mostly failed to guide the leadership to any strategic decisions, were conflicting across the organization, and, in almost all cases, were all reporting as "green."

Working with John and his team, Dana developed a performance management plan that the Director loved. As she went around interviewing mid-level management and communicating the plan, she started to realize the bigger problems with the performance measures within Myopia.org. After several months of hard work, she was able to streamline and align key measures for the leadership and link a dashboard to automated systems that collected the measures. This way, management could not "fudge" the numbers to make themselves look good.

Under John's advice, Kevin and the leadership team used the measures to direct process improvements in a key area of product delivery that was important to customers and was faltering badly. Immediate customer feedback proved their actions had a positive effect. Kevin did not use the measures to punish leadership, but rather, to direct strategic improvement. With success under the initial use of the new performance measurement, Dana was able to get stronger support from the division chiefs and was happy to learn that the branch chiefs applauded the program.

Across Myopia.org, front-line employees and mid-level management began using data to make day-to-day decisions. Dana and John helped each branch, starting with Operations, develop simple operational dashboards and taught employees how to interpret basic charts. After only a small amount of effort, employees across the company were eliminating defects and improving their activities on their own.

Section 4
Understanding How to Change an Organizational Culture

Jim returned to his desk in the sea of cubicles that made up the Pacific Project Management Team. He looked over the documents covered in red ink in front of him--Gwen was at it again. This was the third time she tore up this report and he still had no clearer direction from her. "I'll know it when I see it," she said.

Two weeks prior, Gwen had told him to put together a business development proposal to expand operations in Thailand. That is where Gwen's guidance ended; she did not tell him why, what the purpose was, or even when she expected a response. Jim had seen these taskings before from Gwen, but this was the first time she had tasked him. Most people in the Pacific Branch avoided Gwen because of her poor ability to direct work. Unfortunately, Gwen was representative of how all three Operations branch managers operated. Many across the division were frustrated with the leadership.

Gwen rubbed her hands over her face attempting to massage away the stress and dark circles under her eyes. "What is wrong with these people," she thought to herself after Jim left her office? It seemed that all of the members of the Project Management Team were clueless when it came to putting things together outside of their normal day-to-day work. Jim's third attempt at the Thailand business development proposal was just one of many that frustrated her.

No one on her team seemed to be doing the necessary research to respond to these future-thinking projects, but from her discussions with Ron and Brad in the other branches, it seemed that few of the other project managers had any skills either. Finally, as had become a usual practice for her, Gwen opened the electronic file of what Jim sent her and started working on it herself.

"If you want something done right, you have to do it yourself," she commented aloud to no one in her office. It was going to be another late night.

There is a very appropriate, *albeit fictional,* story of a scientific study where five monkeys were put into a large cage. In the center of the cage was a ladder and at the top of the ladder hung a banana. Every time one of the monkeys started to climb the ladder to get to the banana, all the monkeys were sprayed with cold water. Soon, if one of the monkeys tried to climb the ladder, the other four monkeys would beat up that monkey until finally no monkeys tried to climb the ladder. Then, one of the monkeys was replaced with a new monkey that knew nothing about what was going on in the cage. Immediately, that monkey started to climb the ladder to get the banana and, just as fast, the four other monkeys all attacked him. Over time, every monkey was changed out, until not one monkey existed from the original five who were sprayed with cold water. Regardless, not one monkey would try to climb the ladder to get the banana.

Overall frustration with change, lack of progress, and people not working together are just a few of the symptoms of an ineffective culture. Culture is built over time in reaction to the behaviors of leadership and other employees--like the result of the spraying of monkeys with cold water. The Myopia.org example, featuring Gwen and Jim represents, among other things, a culture of a lack of trust, management solving problems by themselves, and employees stuck in a program and project mentality versus one of problem solving. Myopia.org's culture clearly was created over a long time and it will take a long time to correct.

Like the monkeys in the fictional study above, over time people in the organization do not even know why they do the things they do anymore. In Gwen's case, along with the other managers in Myopia.org, she was not providing clear direction to her staff when she tasked them with challenging assignments that were outside of their day-to-day work. Instead of understanding and discussing what was going on with her staff, she constantly berated them, then did all the work herself. The result was that Gwen found herself heavily overworked and frustrated.

Jim and his counterparts, on the other hand, have settled into a routine of simply doing their project management jobs and not looking at their role as providing customer solutions--just doing and not thinking. To Jim, his efforts felt fruitless and his work was always kicked back, so he put limited effort into the special tasks he was handed and never sought to go above and beyond. Neither of the two in this story communicate their frustrations or desires, which entrenches this behavior even deeper.

An organization's culture will always be demonstrated by the behavior of the people who work in the organization. Regardless of what cultural issues face your organization, the issues have become the norm over time and, in many ways, are hard to identify because it is just the way of the office. Many times, it takes someone from the outside, such as a specialist, to identify the cultural issues and help change the organization. Change management and organizational behavior experts bring many tools and can play a valuable role in instituting change within an organization. Once they identify the cultural norms in an organization, those that are undesirable can then be changed.

An organization can determine its existing cultural issues and norms during its organizational assessment in strategic planning, as discussed earlier. When examining the organization, a keen eye can uncover often unspoken cultural issues. An organization that waits too long to identify the symptoms of Organizational Myopia and address the root causes could find its problems tearing the company apart at the seams.

Much of the "bad culture" found in an organization develops because of a simple lack of understanding between two or more groups. Many times, there are distinctly different cultures that exist within an organization (micro cultures), but neither culture understands the other. Thus, the cultures do not know how to work together.

All organizations will also have competing cultures between the leadership and the employees. This is not surprising, given the motivators that drive people into leadership positions versus those that make a person content with a steady and reliable "X" to "X" job. You can imagine some of the cultural barriers that crop up.

These differences also tend to form between functional and operational sections of a company (e.g., consider the potential differences between Myopia.org's Finance Branch and the Information Branch). It is easy to see how any organization can have many different types of disparate groups that might not get along simply because they do not understand each other.

Regardless of what organization you are examining, there will always be this underlying "culture." Organizational cultures are not inherently bad--they simply represent the way things are. However, many cultures have negative aspects. Once the negative cultural aspects are identified, leadership can focus on changing the behaviors that make up that negative culture.

You may have heard someone--probably a leader--say, "I'm going to change the culture..." Well, the culture is not something someone simply "changes." Cultural change comes from focusing on the behaviors that make up the culture. Understanding where the negative cultural issues exist is the first step.

Next, leadership must establish the organizational values or principles that reflect the culture that they expect of their organization. Values are a key component of an organization's strategic plan as discussed earlier in this book. Sometimes the values already exist, but are simply not being followed, enforced, or modeled.

Leadership, through modeling, must demonstrate the expected behaviors. As well, bringing the various groups together to discuss their differences and understand each other will help to build the much-needed trust that is often lacking. In many cases, experts in change management and organizational behavior can help these troubled organizations.

Sustaining a cultural change usually means consistently measuring the expected behaviors ingrained into the organizational values. Since behaviors are observable actions, where values are loftier aspirations, this is where your measurements should reside. These measures should be adopted into the organization's performance management program and be reviewed by leadership on a regular basis.

As a final example, there was a major company that possessed several admirable cultural aspects and was recognized as one of the best places to work. However, there were a few cultural norms that were not so admirable. For instance, the cultural belief was that if you were not spending money (i.e., on a technology solution), you were not solving problems. Thus, all improvements in the organization tended to be technology solutions and leadership was constantly trying to "get money" to solve problems. This happened, even when no-cost business work was solving more problems than any technology solution could solve. An assessment of the cultural norms within this organization would be a start towards identifying and fixing the problem.

Cultural issues within an organization, both across the organization and between groups, can create significant silo-related issues that are extremely hard to break through. However, with time and effort, organizations can systematically overcome these problems and become even more effective.

Change Readiness versus Change Management

Today, organizations are investing in change management by the droves. The Association for Change Management Professionals and the Change Management Institute have developed a Change Management Body of Knowledge. Prosci has been certifying change managers using the AD-KAR® approach for many years. Many other organizations have created unique approaches to managing change. So, it has become common for organizations to hire change managers and employ them in project and process management.

If you want to change the culture, you need to stop managing change!

It is crazy to hear someone say to stop managing change! However, in today's world, if you are managing change you are behind the power curve. This is because change is almost constant in business today. To keep up with competition, innovation, and regulation (to name just a few of the "tions" that will eat your company for breakfast), you need to move to a level of change readiness.

Consider change readiness to be synonymous with business agility--the ability of your business to rapidly adjust because everyone in that industry is ready and actively looking for ways to positively transform.

The prior Myopia.org example, where Gwen says, "I'll know it when I see it," is an example of a business that is not agile. To be agile, leaders need to accept a level of risk and let their employees try new things. Celebrating failures and promoting appropriate risk leads to an innovative culture that embraces change.

Building a culture of change readiness means that the business moves away from managing change and starts simply changing as part of how it operates. Let us examine change management first, to better understand the difference between change management and change readiness and why change readiness is so important.

Managing change, going back to Kurt Lewin's *Group Dynamic Movement* work, is done essentially in three phases: 1) Pre-Change, 2) Change, and 3) Post-Change. This aligns to Lewin's theory of unfreezing, moving, and refreezing. In order to manage change, the change must occur, or be about to occur, and then change managers react by managing that change. This puts the business in a very reactive and non-agile mode. In today's business world, companies simply cannot keep up with the pace of change.

There are three types of change:

1. Developmental. Developmental change is when an organization makes change over time to promote the evolution of the organization. This type of change is typically referred to as continuous improvement.
2. Transitional. Transitional change is when an organization changes from an old (current) state to a new (defined) state. This is common in mergers and acquisitions, changing business models, adopting a whole new organizational strategy, etc.

3. **Transformational.** This type of change is somewhat like riding a roller coaster. New organizations tend to grow quickly, but often hit a plateau and then decline sharply. Good companies use developmental change (or sometimes transitional change) to develop their business and then start another growth spurt. However, an organization can experience a chaotic decline until it must make a drastic transformational change. This is often referred to as the "Change or Die," situation.

Whether it is developmental, transitional, or transformational, we often start with managing the change effort. Regardless of the why, changes always occur. It is best if organizations operate in a developmental or transitional change environment, because organizations in transformational change are normally in an out-of-control situation.

Anyone who has been involved in change management knows that what is actually being managed is human resistance to change. The act of changing something (e.g., a process, an organizational structure, an operating model, an IT system, etc.) is easy compared to getting people to adopt the change and not derail or stop it. So, becoming change ready and building business agility starts with changing your employees' readiness to change. Adopting a culture of change readiness can help a business avoid becoming overcome with the rate of constant change.

To get a better understanding of change management versus change readiness, think about planting a new lawn.

Your property is full of weeds with hard dirt. Change management is akin to dumping a lot of seed on the surface and spraying it with water hoping that the grass will grow and take root. Change readiness involves more up-front work, but produces better success. Adopting a change readiness approach, would mean removing and killing off all the weeds, tilling the hard dirt, and adding new topsoil. Then, you would spread an even amount of seed and apply regular watering. Chances are, the latter approach would yield a better result. Properly preparing your organization for change versus managing the change when it is thrust upon it is much more effective.

Building a culture that is agile and change ready is a lot easier than one would imagine. It is done in three stages:

1. Building Awareness and Understanding. The first stage is to ensure that your entire company is aware of the business need to be able to change quickly. Many times, organizations do not share with, or are not fully transparent to, their employees when it comes to business strategy, financials, and competitive position. Often, employees are only told the positive aspects of the organization and are "protected" from many of the issues, challenges, and problems the organization faces. Those are left for behind-the-scenes, closed-door meetings and private conference calls.

   At all levels, employees only get part of the story. That is, until it is too late. This is a different type of silo. One that can divide the employees and leadership. Then, when everything "hits the fan" employees are told, and the business begins managing the change.

Providing full transparency and explaining where the organization is and what it faces helps employees at all levels have awareness and understanding of the need for constant change.

2. Obtaining Employee Buy In. Knowing is only half the battle. Once employees understand what is happening inside and outside the organization, they should become positively engaged in helping the organization explore the current situation and look for opportunities to solve problems and improve operations. Sharing everything with the employee base but then telling them, "You got this," stops the change readiness on the spot. So, it is crucial to not only share the organization's status and challenges, but to engage everyone in determining ways in which to respond. This speaks to the importance of employee engagement, discussed later in this section.

3. Preparing Employees with Training & Preparation. Most organizations do a good job of either ensuring people have the training to do their job before they hire them, or making sure they get the training they need to do their job while they are doing the work. Also, many companies ensure their people are trained on things that are important, but ancillary, to their work like regulatory requirements, human resource

issues, and the like. However, to build change readiness, organizations also need to invest in a different type of training for their employees.

Everyone--not just a few--needs to be trained in professional business skills such as strategy, innovation, process improvement, business analytics, and change management. Often, businesses leave this training to specialists within the organization, then deploy them to solve select problems. In these cases, there are never enough people to address all the problems and, often, what is changed and improved does not stick. This is not to say that this expertise is not necessary, but professionals with these skills should transition to more of a coaching and mentoring role for tough problems versus being called in to solve everything.

If an organization can move through these three stages, it can create a culture that not only knows why proactive change is important, but has employees that feel like they can have an active part of that change, have the training and tools that let them make the change, and can identify or know who to call on when they are in over their head. Most of all, leadership within this culture allows for open innovation, constant testing, continuous learning, and steadily getting better.

Employee Engagement Discussion

Since the early 2000's, businesses have focused on employee engagement and its cost to businesses. Virtually any report or study on engagement points out that about 70% of employees in the U.S. are not engaged at work and that is costing businesses upwards of $500 billion a year.

Unfortunately, this employee-focused issue has not changed since before the 1950s when the emphasis was on employee satisfaction. In the 1980s, the emphasis turned to organizational commitment. The business issue; however, has not changed since researchers started studying and quantifying employees' feelings and actions towards their organizations more than 70 years ago.

There are a few major companies out there that have found some success in employee engagement and have become the poster-children for how to treat employees. As in everything else, many companies think that if they simply do the same visible things as those who are successful, they will also be successful, and their survey results will go up. Instead, they need to look at deeper cultural issues to actually effect change and improve their organization.

When you look at this issue from the business' point of view, it does not really care if the employee is "satisfied" at work. It just knows that if the employees are not satisfied, they will not operate as well as they could. What organizations really want is employees "committed" to the organization—i.e. organizational commitment. Employees, on the other hand, do not care about being "committed." What they want is to be "satisfied" with their job—i.e. employee satisfaction. As you can see, the organization and its employees operate in silos based on their expectations.

The concept of "being engaged;" however, is a deeper subject that most companies and employees simply do not understand. Employee satisfaction represents how employees feel about the things they can tangibly measure in their job. Organizational commitment is a result of satisfied employees performing at work, and is measured from the business' point of view. But engagement is something entirely different.

Each of these three terms: satisfaction, commitment, and engagement, work together in business and should not be addressed in silos. Each one is important and should be the focus of employee and organizational wellbeing as a whole.

From a satisfaction point of view, employees are focused on the tangible things that they can measure at work. Things such as the security of their position, commensurate pay and benefits with their role in comparison to others, recognition and rewards, opportunity for advancement, the company dress code, etc.

From an organizational commitment perspective, there are three components: employees, leadership, and the organization. Employees must be present, and they must be dedicated to the work. If the employees are lazy and not interested in working hard--just want to get paid--then they will not be committed. If there is a lack of effective leadership to provide a vision and goals, or reward and recognize employees, then commitment cannot occur. The organization might have people in leadership positions, but they might not be leaders. Lastly, the organization must not just exist, but it needs to be an organization worth being committed to. If your organization does not have a strong purpose, vision, and culture, employees will find it difficult to be committed to it.

Engagement is the term that confuses people the most. That is because it is really based on how employees feel about their job. This is a difficult concept for companies to manage to, so most resort to managing single items that scored low on a survey. Employee satisfaction is easier to manage to because, like the employee, the company can see, touch, and measure it. What confuses an understanding of engagement even further is that many of the surveys that exist today include questions related to commitment and satisfaction as part of the engagement equation.

Employees are basically engaged by four things at work. These four things are: 1) mission or purpose of the company; 2) communication and transparency; 3) leader and employee development; and 4) quality. These things are not obvious to organizations and are usually some of the major problem areas many companies have.

If your company has no or a poor mission/purpose, or it has a good mission/purpose that leaders do not emulate, then why be engaged? It is not about money, or safety, or even recognition. Look at the engagement of 21-years-olds today, who fight and die for their country in the military, for something as simple as "Freedom." They are not paid well, they are afraid a lot of the time, and military personnel get little recognition for their sacrifices. But they do it anyway.

Open and honest, transparent communication builds relationships and trust with leadership and between employees. Most organizations struggle with communication (internal and external). But remember, fear is often driven by the unknown. The more you keep from your employees--whether intentional or not--the more they will distrust you out of fear. Companies need to examine their communication gaps and develop tactics to close those gaps.

Development is more than having classes available or a training budget that no one uses. Development is about actively challenging employees to grow and helping them with the challenge. It is about assisting them to become something better and stronger than they were when they started with the company. If you want to fuel disengagement, keep people doing the same old job every day without developing them to become something bigger and better. Not having a plan for development and not taking actions, or allowing actions, will bore people. Bored employees make disengaged employees.

Quality is a recognition of doing good work, that employees around you are doing good work, and that the management focuses on quality work. If the company does not care, cuts corners, and puts out a shoddy product just to make more money, the employees will be the first to know it. If your company strives--really strives--for quality in everything it does, then employees will buy into that. You will live up to the needs of the customers, deliver things the customer did not even realize it wanted, and do it better than anyone else-

- all the time. Do this and your people will relish being part of a winning team.

So, the discussion needs to turn from one of engagement to one of organizational and employee wellbeing. All things; satisfaction, commitment, and engagement should be evaluated to establish a baseline and then to measure effective improvement. For each of these areas, the organization must focus deeper into the problems that cause a lack of engagement versus focusing only on statements and scores on a survey. Only then will wellbeing occur. Focusing on individual low survey scores addresses the symptom rather than the root cause.

The saying goes, "Culture eats strategy for breakfast." If your culture is one of silos mired in OM, then you will struggle until that culture is changed. Beware of the leader that says she will set out to, "Change the Culture!" Culture is not some dial you can simply turn or a switch you can flip in your organization. It must be analyzed and changed through behavioral tactics.

Much of what is in this book requires a concentrated focus on change. However, change is a scary thing to people-- it takes them out of their comfort zone and creates confusion and worry. All too often these days, we are "managing the change" and companies are becoming overwhelmed. The time for a focus on change readiness is now. Coupled with a highly engaged workforce, change readiness will lead your organization out of OM-crisis.

The Myopia.org strategic team of Dana and John sought out and identified several of the cultural issues that had embedded themselves in the organization over time. They presented their findings to the leadership and after a half-day offsite, they published the first organizational values Myopia.org had ever had. These values were then incorporated into the Myopia.org Strategic Plan. The leadership recognized that they wanted to be "One Team focused on Trust, Honesty, and Credibility." Each word in their new values statement meant something special to the leadership:

__One Team:__ All the disparate groups across Myopia.org understanding each other and working together to service the customer.

__Trust:__ Leaders engaging and empowering employees to come up with innovative solutions; employees and leaders communicating their understanding and expectations on new projects; and employees putting in the right amount of effort when working on special projects.

__Honesty:__ Everyone honestly reporting performance in the organization with the expectation that measures are used to improve the organization and not punish the measurement owners.

__Credibility:__ All Myopia.org employees focused on providing the best service possible; becoming as knowledgeable about their work as possible; and putting the customer first.

Myopia.org's current culture was built over a long time. When interviewed, many of the employees did not even know how it got there. Because Dana identified positive aspects of the culture along with the negative, the organization was able to embark on changing its culture by monitoring and adjusting its behavior.

Kevin looked out the window of his office after reviewing the results of Myopia.ors's quarterly culture assessment. The results still showed a lot of room to grow, but headquarters was pleased with recent customer comments and they liked what they were seeing at Myopia.org.

In Gwen's office, Jim demonstrated an idea to her and the other two branch chiefs on expanding Thailand operations across the organization. Both Gwen and Jim smiled as the others readily accepted their ideas and Gwen heartily congratulated Jim for the great work.

Section 5
Providing Effective Reorganization and Structured Governance

Kevin, Greg, and Stan sat around the small conference room table. They were discussing this week's downturn in market share for the company. As the three stared at the slide on the screen, Greg, who decided to push his retirement out a few years, suggested Kevin shake up the organization again to get things going. Stan defended his support division, inwardly fearing that any reorganization would suck away more of his already strapped resources. Kevin considered his own ideas of swapping Greg and Stan's positions to see what affect it would have, but he kept the ideas to himself. Dana, sitting at the computer, added that maybe they should research the reasons for the downturn first, but was quickly dismissed as she is not truly part of the leadership team.

For a month now, John had sat off to the side of the room, at Kevin's request, evaluating the proceedings of Myopia.org's regular staff meetings. He remained quiet, only taking notes once in a while, mentally preparing himself for his upcoming discussion with Kevin that afternoon. Later that afternoon, Kevin and John sat in Kevin's corner office and Kevin asked for an assessment of how things seem to be going-- what do you think John would say?

When something is wrong and not working in an organization, one of the immediate and recurring reactions of leadership is to break down the "dysfunctional" structure that seems to be causing the root of the problem and start over. As discussed in Parts 1 and 2 of this book, the organizational structure is probably not the problem--the people in it and how they function together is.

Up to this point, Myopia.org has focused its efforts on a multitude of primarily leadership-driven issues. Now, the leadership and employees of Myopia.org need to start operating more like a well-oiled machine. Here are some things you might have noticed from the example above--these are the things John highlighted to Kevin in their follow-up meeting:

1. The Myopia.org leadership meets just about every week for a "staff meeting." Over the past month, John watched them only discuss operational activities affecting Myopia.org for that specific week and the next week. Nowhere in their discussions was there any in-depth assessment of problems or any strategic discussions.

2. The three leaders around the table tend to jump to solutions every week without any details or analysis of the issue. This has caused the organization to change direction on a weekly basis and proves very confusing for the personnel.

3. No one else, aside from Dana and John, has ever attended or presented at the meeting. There never

appears to be any input from the staff on any issue. Even Dana's inputs during the meetings are ignored by the leaders.

4. There never seems to be much structure or agenda to the meetings; no one takes notes, and no actions are documented during or followed up on after the meeting.

Corporate Governance

All organizations have an organizational structure, but often organizations lack any true "organization." Hence, the above issues are commonly present. It might be that the solution to an organization's problems is to adopt a new structure, but that should only happen after the problems have been examined and the adoption of the new structure is thoughtfully planned and implemented. In most cases, what the organization lacks is any type of formal corporate governance--a topic touched on in previous sections.

Corporate governance is, at its core, nothing more than simple and documented rules on business processes, customs, policies, laws, and structures affecting the way a business is directed, administered, and controlled. Many authors describe corporate governance in terms of a system of structuring, operating, and controlling a company with a view to do the following:

▸ Achieving long term strategic goals
▸ Satisfying shareholders, creditors, employees, customers, partners, and suppliers

▶ Complying with the legal and regulatory requirements

Some examples of structures that make up corporate governance are: a strategic board of directors; change management boards; working groups and planning teams; centers of excellence and communities of practice; as well as how an organization is matrixed.

How an organization is governed is determined by how it is controlled and managed. There are two types of governance--centralized and decentralized.

▶ Control is who is making or setting the business processes, customs, policies, rules, and structures
▶ Manage is who is enforcing the business processes, customs, policies, rules, and structures
▶ Centralized means it exists as a specific group in the organization
▶ Decentralized means that it exists across the organization

The military, for instance, tends toward centralized control and decentralized execution (management). In the United States Air Force, all of the major commands have similar corporate governance policy. Most identify the corporate board (decision making body), standing teams that evaluate and report on key areas important to the organization (like finance or information technology), and how information flows within the organization horizontally and laterally.

In the Joint and Army circles, a process was developed and used by some called "Boards, Bureaus, Centers, Cells, and

Working Groups (B2C2WG)." This process outlines what types of groups should be formed and for what purpose. It can be very effective when understood and applied correctly.

Most of this seems like it is common sense, but all too often the weekly "staff meeting" syndrome takes over and operations ends up ruling the daily life of the organization. Thus, the first step to breaking away from the doldrums of a strictly operational focus in your organization, is to develop a strategic and effective corporate structure that ensures that everyone's voice is heard at all levels (*shown in Figure 6*).

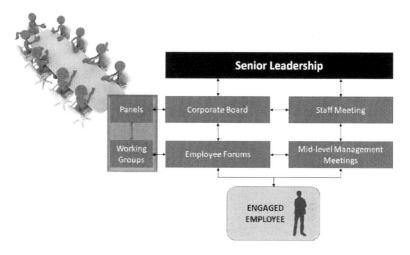

Figure 6: Sample Governance Structure

At the leadership level, there should be two bodies--operational and strategic. The operational body deals with the tactical (day-to-day) and operational (annual) activities of the organization and should meet on a regular basis (weekly or bi-weekly is best for most organizations). This meeting should be focused on identifying and discussing problems normally identified through performance measurement. These problems are then passed onto separate teams to work. Finally, leadership makes decisions on results and recommendations from the teams. If leadership spends its time solving day-to-day problems during weekly meetings without engaging the staff, the solutions leadership develops will not work.

Strategically, leadership should meet quarterly to review measurement trends, discuss strategic planning implementation progress, direct major process improvements linked to strategy, and make strategic decisions. Annually, this body should review and update the strategic plan following the guidance from the strategic planning section of this book.

The memberships of these two governance bodies are essentially the same. However, the purposes of these two bodies are wholly different.

Below the leadership level, at least one mid-level management team should exist to discuss and present items to leadership for discussion and decision. This is the body through which issues which affect the worker are carried forward to leadership. Also, these teams pass decisions and information down to employees. To the side of this structure, specialized (standing and ad hoc) teams work on specific items, such as finance or budget, information technology, marketing and communications, and operational excellence. With proper corporate governance structure, most any organization can operate effectively. The major task is to define the decision-making roles and communication flows of an organization through matrixed teams.

Meeting Effectiveness

One of the most talked about issues, when it comes to management, is effective meetings. In a recent book search on Amazon.com, there were over 10,000 titles listed discussing "effective meetings" in one way or another. Aligned to a defined corporate governance, effective meeting management is key. Having effective meetings is really very simple. The most important thing is to ensure everyone in the organization is aware of, understands the value of, and knows how to hold effective meetings. Here are three basic items of effective meetings that are often missed:

1. Have an Agenda: Every meeting should have a written agenda that outlines the purpose, what will be discussed, what decisions are required, and the times associated with the meeting (start, stop, and topic discussion). This simple meeting pre-planning tool makes a world of difference in running effective meetings. Making this a requirement in your organization is paramount.

2. Taking Minutes: Without fail, someone in every meeting should record the discussion, the decisions, and the tasks that result from a meeting. These minutes should be shared with everyone present and anyone not present that might have an interest or stake in the team's meeting. An effective way to provide full transparency to standing team meetings is to

establish a shared folder of some type for that team and post the completed minutes from every meeting in that folder.

3. Accountability. Following up on tasks from meetings is key to making meetings effective. Ensure the tasks are clearly assigned in the meeting minutes and ensure the open tasks are reviewed in follow-up meetings. Do not let unfinished tasks just "drop off" the list. Have a process to close tasks where the team approves closing items versus making it one person's responsibility.

Toastmasters International is an excellent training resource for learning how to run effective meetings. If your organization is large enough, consider starting a closed club at your office. If not, most communities have several clubs that your employees can join. If you support Toastmasters, recognize active participation by your personnel by allowing them the time to attend meetings, recognizing that attendance on assessments, and promoting participation at work. For business, Toastmasters is like sending someone to a very inexpensive year-round class from which you can see immediate results.

Reorganization

Not all problems stem from ineffective meetings. Some organizations do need to reorganize their organizational structure. If so, it is because the organizational structure is not effective with the current mission and business processes. Reorganizing to "shake things up," seldom works.

When reorganizing, there are specific steps an organization should take to ensure it reorganizes for the right reasons and that the reorganization is effective the first time. When reorganizing, one critical mistake organizations often make is to organize around people--giving people a job. A business should be organized around its mission and purpose, not around people that work within the organization. Here is a simple set of steps for effectively reorganizing your myopic organization:

1. Determine how the new company structure will be organized; around the purpose, mission, major processes, the market, or customers. This is the first step in any reorganization and should focus on people within the organization. If the people you currently have in your organization do not fit into the new structure, then why are they working in your company?

2. Next, design your organizational structure. All organizations have different levels of employees, managers, and leaders. These levels can be prominently defined in strictly hierarchical organizations, or can be less well defined in flatter organizations. Also, organizations can be structured to be strictly functional, divisional, mixed, or matrixed. Regardless of what it looks like; the key is how it operates. Proper corporate governance is important to an effective business! The critical aspect here is that the company can effectively deliver around its primary focus (purpose, mission, processes, market, or customers).

3. Once you have the structure designed, determine the required manpower positions to operate in that structure. This includes appropriate levels, skills, competencies, and span of control. Consider the availability for growth and development in the new structure. Ensure that there are enough opportunities for building new leaders within the organization and that you have not eliminated that possibility with the positions (or lack of positions) created.

4. Next, put people in the positions you created in your new organization. Sometimes people do not have the skills required to fill the roles to which they are assigned. This is ok, but creates immediate learning opportunities to develop the required knowledge, skills, and abilities to perform the job. An organization should look at leadership and staff separately when assigning personnel to positions because of required competencies.

5. The final step involves all the administrative aspects of an organizational change. It requires rearranging the physical structure of the organization to match what has been built on paper. This includes moving people, furniture, and equipment; acquiring new property or divesting old; and updating phone systems and rosters.

When your senior staff is not meeting strategically, lacks governance, and makes knee-jerk organizational changes driven by personnel and not mission, you need to look to improve the governance structures and meeting processes before reorganizing. Simply knocking down silos that have been built over many years will only cause operational disruption, upset personnel, and destroy productivity. If reorganization is required to meet purpose, mission, processes, market, or customers, it should be done systematically and smartly.

JOHN KNOTTS

After Kevin and John met and discussed what John saw over the past month, they developed a game plan. Along with Dana, Kevin calls in the Myopia.org division and branch leadership. They first discuss how they are organized and the need for a defined governance structure as well as some education and training for the staff on proper meeting effectiveness. Three working groups are formed to review the current organizational structure, develop a governance approach, and develop training.

In two weeks, the organizational structure working group returns to the weekly staff meeting to report on a possible reorganization. It was determined that reorganizing Myopia.org was not required at this time, but in working with human resources, the team was better able to define the roles and responsibilities and required competencies for the entire staff. They are adding this to the education and training agenda. Also, the governance structure working group presented three courses of action for leadership to review and decide upon.

A month later, leadership approved a new Myopia.org Corporate Governance document, presented by the working group, that defined two leadership teams (corporate council and operational board), created a branch chief forum, established three permanent advisory panels (budget and finance, information technology, and human resources), and outlined guidance for establishing ad hoc working groups.

After communicating the new guidance, educating the staff, and enforcing the structure and procedures, Myopia.org

146

found that communication and collaboration across the organization improved dramatically. Stan, and his branch chiefs from the Support Division, all feel more engaged in operational activities. Operation's personnel also reported feeling more involved in strategic decisions in the company.

Section 6
Promoting Customer-focused Cross-functionality Through Process Management

John was walking around the offices of Myopia.org one day, quietly reviewing the organizational efficiency. Earlier that week, Greg, the Operations Division Chief, asked him to take a look at the way the operation ran to see if he could find efficiencies within the Operations Division. During their initial meeting, Greg took John around to meet all the branch chiefs while explaining how Operations ran. The branch chiefs each proudly pointed out the past process improvements their teams had made, many of which, to John, seemed to be familiar across the Division, but implemented differently.

The Division was broken into three branches: Americas, European, and the Pacific Rim. Each branch had its own team of operators consisting of sales, project management, contracting, and delivery execution. Organizationally, the Division was spread out into four separate sections on two floors of Myopia.org's headquarters building. The Americas Branch operated out of two sections on the first floor and the overseas branches had some people on the first floor but most of their operations worked on the second floor. The Division was operating from about four in the morning to nine at night to accommodate the various time zones Myopia.org supported. Within each branch, the teams were broken even further into offices that handled geographic parts of their territory--each office was made up of an individual team of sales, project management, contracting, and delivery execution.

John noted throughout the day that some offices were very busy, and others were not. Also, those on the Americas Branch who came in during the hours of 8 am and 5 pm, seemed to have all the additional duties and special projects for the company. As John dug a little deeper into the operation, he discovered that each of the branches relied on the Finance Branch in the Support Division to review its customer projects.

Finance was broken up into two offices--Operations and Support. The Support Office provided organizational-wide financial support to Myopia.org, while the Operations Office supported activities in the Operations Division. Of course, the Information Branch and the People Branch of the Support Division supported everyone in the Operations Division, but they did not feel they were involved in the day-to-day, customer-facing operation.

Many branch and team chiefs in the Operations Division saw everyone in the Support Division as less than helpful. After about a week, John was prepared to sit down with Greg and discuss his findings--what do you think he will say?

As an organization grows, silos start to form. When an organization is new and small, everyone chips in and does a little of everything. The owner is usually involved in everything from human resources, to product development and delivery, to sales and marketing. In these small organizations, you seldom see issues that normally come with silos. However, as the organization starts to grow, "departments" and "teams" start to form to handle the workload. It is natural and expected for any organization. Within these organizational entities appear "walls." We have already seen how these walls affect other parts of an organization, but one of the biggest silos is across processes. With these silos can come redundancy, ineffectiveness, and inefficiency.

Two major types of silos form within organizations--divisional and functional. Divisional silos form within the operational activities of the organization when you break up the operation to support segments of your customer population, or to take advantage of operational differences such as time zones. In Myopia.org, the Operations Division is broken into three primary silos with a geographic focus--Americas, Europe, and the Pacific area. Finance also has two divisional silos--Operations and Support.

Functional silos form both outside and inside the operations of a company through the support of functional specialization. In the individual operational offices of Myopia.org, each team is further broken into specialists in the functional areas of sales, project management, contracting, and execution. The Support Division has three major functional silos--Finance, Information, and People.

The most important lesson from this book is that there is nothing you can do about eliminating these silos from your organization! In the past, Myopia.org tried to improve its operation by breaking down some of these silos, reorganizing, and moving leadership around. However, the silos never went away and, thus, neither did the problems associated with them. Greg's gut reaction to any problems within the Operational Division might be to reorganize his entire division, or Kevin's action might be to reorganize the entire company again. But, in the long run, this will not overcome the organizational problem and will only confuse, scare, and irritate employees.

From a process perspective, those inside the silos need to better understand what problems are caused by having silos and how they can overcome them. This will help. There are three major ways to overcome OM within an organization's processes: 1) By providing a customer focus to everyone in the organization; 2) By focusing on and controlling the centralized processes; and 3) By instilling a culture of continuous process improvement.

Customer Focus: Almost everyone in business understands the concept of customer-focus. If your company does not know who its customer is, then the problems you have with process management and process improvement run much deeper than silos. Many times; however, the various divisional and functional silos are only focused on their "own" customers. This often causes confusion across an organization and its processes--we have seen this in performance measurement.

In the case of Myopia.org, the three branches and multiple geographic offices each have individual customers around the world. Within the offices, the roles of sales, project management, contracting, and delivery execution only focus on the immediate customer--the next step in the process. In the case of the three branches in the Support Division, they have their own internal customers they concern themselves with.

Below is the list of customers that John identified to Greg at the end of his assessment (*see Table 2*):

Table 2: Myopia.org Customer Focus Assessment	
ORGANIZATIONAL ELEMENT	**CUSTOMERS**
Operations Division	▸ Kevin, Myopia.org Director ▸ Operations Branches
Geographic Operations Branch	▸ Operations Division ▸ Geographic Offices ▸ Geographic External Customers
Geographic Office	▸ Geographic Offices ▸ Office Team Members ▸ Geographic External Customers
Sales Personnel	▸ Geographic Offices ▸ Sales Managers ▸ Office Team Members ▸ Geographic External Customers
Project Management Personnel	▸ Geographic Offices ▸ Project Management Offices ▸ Office Team Members ▸ Geographic External Customers
Contracting Personnel	▸ Geographic Offices ▸ Legal and Contractual ▸ Regulation Entities ▸ Office Team Members ▸ Geographic External Customers

ORGANIZATIONAL ELEMENT	CUSTOMERS
Delivery Execution Personnel	▶ Geographic Offices ▶ Execution Management ▶ Office Team Members ▶ Geographic External Customers
Support Division	▶ Kevin, Myopia.org Director ▶ Operations Division ▶ Support Branches
Finance Branch	▶ Myopia.org ▶ Support Division ▶ Geographic Offices ▶ Financial Regulation External Entities
Information Branch	▶ Myopia.org ▶ Support Division ▶ Information Technology Regulation Entities
People Branch	▶ Myopia.org ▶ Support Division ▶ Human Resource Regulation External Entities

As you can see, across Myopia.org, and like many other organizations, everyone in the organization has several competing customers and some similar or overlapping customers. Customers are recognized by each part of Myopia.org. This could be the same customer, but at different levels, or totally different customers. The key is, each part of Myopia.org has a customer.

The most important customer for Myopia.org is that *external geographic customer*. That customer should be at the top of everyone's list of customers. Unfortunately, many times this is not the case. In some cases, especially in functional parts of an organization, the ultimate customer might not even be a consideration in the day-to-day operations.

For example, the People Branch of Myopia.org sees its customers as the organization, its division leadership, and external entities such as the employees' union. Nowhere in its consideration does it see itself supporting Myopia.org's external geographic customer. However, the whole reason the People Branch exists is to ensure Myopia.org can meet the needs of the external customer because the external geographic customer is what drives the work for Myopia.org and the reason the organization exists at all. Without Myopia.org customers, there would be no Myopia.org and, hence, no People Branch. When people and entities within the organization lose focus on the ultimate customer they stop working together and start working toward their own goals and objectives, serving different masters.

Re-education and constant reminders, at all levels of the organization, of who the customers are for each part of the end-to-end process, and who the ultimate customer is, proves to be the most important exercise any organization can engage itself in. When everyone knows who the various customers are and focuses on the most important customer first, they start to operate more as a team. When the water boy of a football team focuses his job on beating the other team versus giving water to the team players, everyone on the team is stronger.

There are two valuable process-related mapping techniques that help organizations do this: 1) Value chain analysis, and 2) SIPOC mapping.

At the highest level of the organization, a value chain should be developed that outlines the major operations from a customer's perspective and identifies the supporting elements of the value chain. Only one value chain exists for an organization, but the perspective of the value chain might change within different areas of large organizations. Some organizations, made up of several separate organizations, could feasibly have different value chains.

At the process level, identification of the customer in the process is best accomplished by mapping a process at the SIPOC-level: Suppliers, Inputs, Processes, Outputs, and Customers. This Lean Six Sigma, high-level process mapping tool is an important first step to understanding the flow of processes within an organization and who is important at every step. The SIPOC map should align with the overall value chain for the organization. Often, people map their processes without regard to how they fit within the overall organization's operation--silo!

Asking some simple questions about operational concerns can highlight a poor customer focus. If your information technology department is only focused on the bandwidth of its Internet, help desk phone response, and the storage size of the servers, it may leave out the needs of the customers that drive the need of the information technology equipment in the first place. In that case, they have lost focus. If your human resources or legal departments are only focused on meeting regulatory requirements and improving their internal systems, chances are they have lost emphasis on what is important. When operational sections are competing against each other versus working together, or simply "throwing work over the fence" for someone else to deal with (i.e., sales to product development to shipping), it is clear they are not truly customer-focused.

It is very easy for OM to form and people to become myopic in their view of the operation. Each team's vision of what is needed focuses on the task in front of it and not the reason for its existence in the first place. It is almost as if the teams are constantly operating in a "knife fight" situation. As you can imagine, refocusing everyone's attention on the end customer can be a lot easier than reorganizing the company for the "nth" time.

Centralized Processes: Commonly, an organization that completes a strong value chain analysis and related SIPOC analysis will be able to quickly see processes across an organization start to link together. Additionally, the organization may identify several stand-alone and a few primary processes that impact different segments of that organization. Enter Business Process Management (BPM).

All organizations are made up of hundreds of linked and stand-alone processes that drive their day-to-day activities. Some of these processes may be replicated over-and-over within the organization, without most of the employees even realizing they are following the same processes. Often, an organization's employees will comment that, "We have to do things differently for this type of work or this customer," but in reality, the processes may be practically identical. When broken down to an activity-level, all the different processes start to look the same.

Consider the infamous "meeting." If you talk to one person, they will go on-and-on about the meetings they go to and how each meeting is different and the meetings they attend are nothing like the meetings other people in the organization attend. But let us look at what really makes up a meeting: it has a purpose; it has an agenda; it has an organizer, a leader, and other roles; it follows a time schedule; its members make decisions; it has minutes; and it has follow-up. Well, at least the good meetings look like this--the bad ones might occur without an agenda or minutes, where no one knows what they are doing there and why they are even in attendance, and there are no actions or follow-up. Everyone in an organization attends meetings every day. Would you like the meetings you attend to be productive?

The good meeting example above demonstrates that, at the activity-level, many processes are very similar. By understanding an organization's processes at the value chain- and SIPOC-level, and then breaking them down to a process-mapped-level, you begin to see the activities that make up the various processes and the redundancies across the organization. Also, you start to focus on things such as similar and disparate customers, aligned measures, and a common vision. Effective centralization of processes begins with taking a solid process inventory, then mapping out the processes to a level that allows for effective understanding.

Once you have a solid foundational understanding of what an organization does--process-wise--you can start to strategically improve the organization. As you may have noted from John's observations above, he was briefed on several process improvement projects across the organization that all seemed very repetitive in nature. Why is this? This is what happens when no one understands what is going on in other silos and no one sees the similarity of processes across the organization. With an effective catalog of processes, Myopia.org would see how similar its processes are and could potentially replicate a process improvement implemented for one area across the entire enterprise. Also, if it has a single process that everyone follows for something like sales, for instance, then they would only improve that single sales process, versus multiple similar sales processes. This eliminates the wasted effort of multiple process improvement activities achieving similar, yet redundant, outcomes.

Additionally, when the organization understands and measures all its processes, it better understands which processes are more important than others, which processes are in trouble, and which processes are working fine. This provides leadership with the ability to strategically select which processes it desires to improve over others to appropriately commit resources (i.e., time and money). Can you imagine the cost of the several branches across Myopia.org all conducting the same process improvement over-and-over again?

The goal is not to stop process improvement by the employees, but to ensure that leadership controls the improvement of processes when an expenditure of resources is required. For example: everyone in Myopia.org working similar process improvements involving personnel from the Information Branch could tie up the few information technology personnel available on multiple process improvement activities. Instead, leadership could dedicate one person to a high-priority process that is replicated across the organization's similar processes.

Additionally, if an improvement solution results in the development of some type of automated database or system, the organization can end up with several home-grown data systems that probably fail to talk to each other. Often, these actions occur by individual sections contracting out work to others to build information solutions to "fix their problem." This causes an immediate drain on precious resources, but also maintenance and changes over the years can cause additional significant resource costs. In most cases, these home-grown systems fail to work together, which eventually creates another type of silo--the information technology silo.

Culture of Continuous Process Improvement: Another form of silo in an organization occurs with respect to process improvement when the company dedicates a small team to do all process improvements. The organization only formally trains and certifies a few personnel as Lean Six Sigma and Change Management practitioners because the costs prohibit fully training and certifying everyone across the organization. Then, these few try to take on the brunt of the process improvement work for the organization by themselves. This creates a limited resource that is often grossly overworked, saddled with tremendous responsibilities and priorities, and has little grassroots impact on the organization.

Successful process improvement in an organization is best performed through the development of a *culture of continuous process improvement*. The first most crucial aspect of a culture of process improvement is engaged leadership. Without a strong leadership focus on process improvement, most proposed activities will fall upon deaf ears. This also means that leadership must give more than "lip service" to an organization's process improvement efforts--it must be involved.

Of course, any organization that hopes to have an effective process improvement program must also have some well-trained "change agents." Without Lean Six Sigma Master Black, Black, and Green Belts (or similarly trained and experienced individuals), leading major process improvements and guiding, coaching, mentoring, and training personnel, it is difficult to have an effective process improvement program.

The third critical aspect of a strong culture of continuous process improvement is to involve <u>all employees</u>. This means the training and guidance in process improvement methods and techniques does not stop with the practitioners. You must make a point to involve all employees in process improvement projects, provide just-in-time training, and recognize the efforts of individuals and teams. This type of employee involvement does not have to be extremely formal and the training does not need to be very in-depth. Simply get employees to start thinking about process flow, areas of waste and non-value-added work, and how to measure what they do every day. Soon, you will see them start to identify and fix problem areas on their own.

The quality concept, mainly found in manufacturing, of the "andon cord" is a perfect example of process improvement at the employee level. In a manufacturing-like environment, if an employee "on-the-line" discovers a defect in the product, they are expected to "stop the process" by pulling on a cord or signaling through an andon device. Then everyone quickly examines the defect, determines the root cause, fixes the process, and restarts the operation. This system ensures that defects are not passed down the line until quality control discovers it (if they ever do).

Stopping the process does not have to occur immediately. In Toyota plants, if an assembly line worker discovers a defect, he or she signals using the andon system and then removes a magnet from his or her helmet and attaches it to the area of the defect. Work continues on the designated process, while a supervisor immediately responds and assesses the situation. The supervisor switches out his or her own magnet for the employee's magnet and then he or she "owns" the problem. If the defect cannot be solved before the next step in the process, the line is stopped, and the problem is worked on by a full team. It is not uncommon to hear andon "music" playing across a Toyota plant, which signals its commitment to just-in-time problem solving.

This same concept can be used effectively in a service-oriented business. How many times in a paper process do we push a product from one office to the next without it being defect free? Too often is probably your answer. In these service-oriented, paper-based processes, we need to institute and allow for the introduction of virtual "andon cords." Then, when someone in the chain receives something that is not as expected, instead of sending it back for corrections, he or she can stop the process and meet with the stakeholders to fix the process once and for all.

Through leadership support, project mentorship, and engaged employees, process improvement efforts occur without much effort. The best process improvement programs allow time in the work schedule to focus on solving process-related problems. Strong and engaged leadership, well-trained change champions, and empowered employees make for an effective continuous process improvement culture.

Silos always form, and OM can be particularly destructive within processes. Understanding customers, through value chain analysis and SIPOC development helps focus the entire organization on the key customers. Centralization of processes with an end-to-end catalog eliminates redundancy and guides process improvement efforts. And, building a culture of continuous improvement engages employees in the day-to-day business of improvement without simply relying on a few highly-trained experts.

Greg quickly saw the merits of John's findings and sat down with his fellow leaders to discuss and champion a strategic approach to building a continuous improvement culture in Myopia.org. Due to the size of the organization, Myopia.org formally established one Lean Six Sigma Master Black Belt, two Black Belts, and six Green Belts across the organization. The Master Black Belt position was aligned to work with Dana, while the Black and Green Belts were spread across the organization, but matrixed back to Dana's section for the purpose of organized process improvement and reporting.

Within six months, a formal process management program was established in Myopia.org. The business had a complete process catalog, a strong understanding of the high-level processes across the company, and performance measures aligned to all the key organization-wide processes. Leadership instituted just-in-time training programs and general educational activities for employees in the areas of process improvement, performance management, problem solving, and change management. Myopia.org embarked on strategic process improvement activities and involved key external stakeholders and customers in its improvement activities.

John sat down with Greg over lunch a year after his initial analysis. Together they reviewed return on investment reports from several process improvement projects and discussed future efforts that would propel Myopia.org closer toward its strategic vision that had previously been developed. Greg leaned back with a smile on his face as he thought back *to the day John had out-briefed him on his findings and analysis. They had come a long way, process-wise, in Myopia.org.*

Section 7
Fair and Equitable Resource Distribution

John was invited to the end-of-year resource review with the Myopia.org leadership team. In preparation for the meeting, he reviewed the organizational assessment he had done when building the strategy. He then set up a meeting with Silvia, the Chief of the Financial Management Branch.

When John arrived for the meeting, he found Silvia and her staff just finishing up what appeared to be a very stressful discussion involving many spreadsheets and reports. As the meeting broke up, Silvia's staff quickly hurried back to their respective desks, each carrying armloads of reports to immediately work on.

"The Division Chiefs just don't get it," Silvia complained as they started their discussion. "They must think that money grows on trees around here," she lamented. Throughout the hour-long meeting, Silvia continued to highlight all the challenges she faced at this time of year when the annual budget was discussed and ratified. The crux of the conversation kept coming back to her belief that no one outside of her office knew where money was spent or how much was being spent. To her, the rest of the organization simply didn't care, and they just wanted more and more for their pet projects that, in her mind, did not seem all that important.

During the resource review the following week, John sat quietly at the end of the conference room table as the leaders of Myopia.org argued about how much other divisions, branches, or offices received for things like manpower, budget, and technology and how little they were receiving in comparison. Since John had been working successfully with the leadership team for a while now, they all turned to him for advice.

In any relationship, personal or business, money is usually the leading cause of stress. Myopia.org's predicament is undoubtedly similar to you have experienced in many organizations you have worked with or in--perhaps even the one you are in now. Every organization works within a finite budget for resources, and budget allocation seldom is as much as the people in the organization would like. A result of a deeply-siloed organization is that the various silos often bicker openly--sometimes behind others' backs--about the inequity of resource distribution within the organization.

In many ways, it is simply not possible to solve this issue...you cannot magically add more money to the organization. So, it is important to ensure resource allocation is done in a structured, fair, and transparent manner. Resources that are often considered critical to siloed departments are money, people, information technology (hardware and software), and infrastructure (facility and equipment). These things are generally fought over in that order.

Structured resource allocation can take many forms. Strict industrial engineering practices can determine defensible resource needs for measurable work, but much of today's business labor has become harder-and-harder to quantify. Activity based costing methodologies can help an organization understand allocation and costs, but sometimes fall short of showing the actual resource needs. To get to a structured approach, the organization must ensure that what it is doing is focused on the mission of the organization and it needs to understand the processes associated with the work being done. Developing resource productivity and capacity models and systems can help quantify and manage the workload.

The most important thing about a structured approach to resource management is to get everyone to understand and agree upon the approach. It is very easy for organizational leaders and employees to blame the "system" for the resource issues they perceive they have versus accepting and adopting the resource allocation. An organization should take its time to develop a single approach and employ that approach across the entire organization. The system or systems employed should provide metrics that roll up to the highest reporting level and drill down to the lowest level. Organizations that employ different resource determination means across the company, without regard to integration and interconnectivity, will create even deeper silos. Consider employing an enterprise-wide approach that everyone understands and agrees with when adopting your resource determination methodologies.

Fair can mean many things to many people. The fair approach to some might mean an equal distribution of resources across an organization. Your resource determination methodology should provide your company with an accurate assessment of your true resource needs. Your budget will inform your company of your actual resources. The focus should be to balance true needs with actual resources to come up with an effective approach. Leadership must see how its work fits into the strategy of the organization, everyone needs to agree on the priority of organizational functions as well as the impact of underfunded programs. In all organizations, there are critical efforts that must be resourced at or near 100%--sometimes even over 100%. Also, in all organizations, there are efforts that can operate with less than required funding, at least for a short period.

So, what should be funded at 100% when other things go underfunded? Organizational leadership must look to the strategy to determine where they will prioritize money and resources. By doing this as a leadership team, everyone understands where funds are being spent and why. Using a pairwise ranking approach can help organizations effectively prioritize their resource related requirements against each other.

The determination methodology will demonstrate the impact of a lesser resource allocation than that being sought, or what is perceived to be required. As a leadership team, everyone should agree with the strategy as to where the organization's priorities lie and what can suffer if need be. Then, the resources are allocated in a more responsible manner that is fair to the business. If each silo fails to elevate its point of view to a higher strategic level, everyone will constantly fight and argue about the current allocation. Understanding what is fully funded and what is funded less than required against an agreed upon standard makes it difficult for leadership to complain.

Organizations may have many strategic needs that require a full-funding emphasis. Perhaps regulatory compliance has significantly increased, and money needs to be dedicated to becoming compliant with the new laws before being fined or shut down. Perhaps the organization has grown very quickly and needs to prioritize funds to improve and automate processes or hire more staff to meet capacity. Maybe the organization is falling behind in product innovation and needs a greater emphasis on research and development. All too often, organizations face all these issues, and several others, at once. Thus, it is important to prioritize all items so that the organization can focus and not become disjointed. When an organization does not evaluate everything, when making resource decisions, it may tend to "switch gears" several times during the year to address the next big issue or crisis.

Separate financial management functional departments often exist within organizations. Financial management, like human resources and legal, is a special skill set. Accordingly, financial management tends to be inherently siloed. Even startup businesses, which rarely begin with silos, often employ outside assistance in this area to handle the various difficult financial management activities, which require special skills and knowledge and create this financial management silo.

The focus on customer, as discussed earlier, is important when considering resource distribution and financial management. Chief financial officers and finance departments often focus on the shareholder as the customer rather than the end customer being served by the business. This emphasis by finance on a dramatically different customer can create a very significant silo in the organization. The challenge becomes whether a company is working to provide valuable products and services to its customers, or it is focused on providing return on investment to its shareholders. Finance often considers itself as the "honest broker" in these situations, looking out for the investors and, in doing so, can work against the mission and purpose of the organization.

Human resources and financial management practitioners often have a language and methodology of their own. How they do things can seem like a mysterious "black box" to outsiders, where one thing goes in and magically something different comes out. And, many times, finance, because of its importance to the business and to the business stakeholders, begins to direct the actions of the business itself. In some cases, because of a lack of transparency, the finance department can unknowingly destroy a company when it has too much control.

Thus, the last aspect of a successful resource allocation program that overcomes OM is full transparency in the methodology used and in the allocation of resources. Publishing through shared locations, websites, and clear communication of the resource determination and allocation made by the leadership, as well as why such decisions were made, will go a long way to educating middle management and employees about the direction of the company. This action of open and honest reporting not only eliminates the backroom discussions about the "haves" and "have-nots", but also is effective at educating the employees about resource determination and management.

One of the biggest problems with resource utilization and allocation in a siloed organization is caused by the constant attempt by leaders to grow their "piece of the pie" by proposing to take over functions currently outside of their control. If it is not clear who owns a process, some leaders will try to take that process and build resources around it. This is not always a bad thing. However, to avoid any such confusion or grabs for power, top leadership can clearly establish process boundaries and ownership when the resource determination methodology is built.

By reviewing the allocation quarterly, and the system itself annually, leadership will continue to understand and accept the current structure. If the system makes sense and leadership agrees to it, each faction of the business can expend its energy every year on the work that matters and not on how the leaders can grow their empire. By aligning spending to an organization's strategic direction, "pet projects," who "screams the loudest," and the "squeaky wheels" are not automatic winners in the resource determination process.

To that same end, once money is allocated, holding executives accountable is extremely important. There are few things worse than one part of the company going over budget without anyone doing anything about it. When one leader's planned efforts do not get funded to the level she expected and she decides to spend the money regardless, she must be held accountable. Otherwise, soon, everyone will start to ignore their prescribed budgets and justify (to themselves) why they are over-spending on what they deem important. The moment someone starts ignoring her budgetary constraints, senior leadership should step in and stop the activity. Running unchecked, the business is doomed to failure.

Thus, maintaining a transparent resource determination and allocation approach that is fair and equitable to the organization and holding leadership accountable for staying within their prescribed resource allocation is key to overcoming OM. Leadership standing behind the resourcing decisions made and sticking to the decisions without changing course repeatedly throughout the year will ensure the success of the approach.

John's recommendations aligned with Myopia.org's strategic planning efforts and became a major action item for the organization to focus on as it went through its journey. Over two years, the organization's manpower, finances, and technology processes evolved into a structured, fair, and transparent approach. Employees at all levels were engaged to make Myopia.org's approach an industry standard and best in class. Even a core team from Myopia.org presented their results at several conferences in the years following.

Myopia.org's leaders found that, although not everything they wanted was funded right away, they understood why and were able to share this with their department personnel. Future resource reviews started moving considerably smoother and Sylvia and her team became more engaged in the organization's mission.

Section 8
Communication as a Key to Overcoming Organizational Myopia

Myopia.org, although not a union-based organization, holds a monthly employee meeting. The employee meeting is a non-management event where employees raise their concerns and issues to an internally-elected group. These elected leaders carry the concerns and issues to Kevin, the Director of Myopia.org. John was impressed by these events when he did his organizational assessment and received permission to attend the meetings with Kevin to better understand employee issues.

One of the first things John learned was that most of the employee issues brought up in the monthly meetings were not making it to the leadership team. This was not totally the fault of the elected employee leadership, but more a prioritization and time-relation issue. Since Kevin only set aside a half an hour each month to meet with the employee leadership team, they only brought up the most important items on their list. Additionally, these confidential communications were normally kept at Kevin's level and there was no follow-up on any required actions. Lastly, John noted that several of the items would be easily fixed if the employees simply heard more from Kevin directly, but since this system was in place, he only interacted with them through the employee leadership team.

John also noted, during his assessment of Myopia.org, that other internal and external communication issues seem to exist. When it came to Operations, one Branch seldom spoke to another on a regular basis and even within teams, communications were hampered. Most of the employees did not even know what other sections of the company even did. This seemed to create a lot of confusion and concerns when it came to managing end-to-end processes within the organization.

Externally, Myopia.org had a website, and was taking advantage of some social media by setting up a Facebook and Twitter site. After a quick review of the Myopia.com's external online presence, John easily saw that it had not been updated in several months at least. Coupled with the boxes of strategic plans in Dana's office, it was clear there was not a great deal of external customer communication activity. In fact, no one in Myopia.org was responsible for communication--internally or externally.

As Mypia.org was developing its strategic plan, John obviously had some specific recommendations regarding communication.

Unfortunately, in many organizations, especially those having trouble, you will find an overwhelming lack of communication. Sure, people are talking, but messages are undoubtedly mixed, the content is usually old, and there is probably a lot more rumor than fact. Also, in many organizations, internal employee communications and external customer communications have not kept up with technology. Moreover, what communication is occurring is seldom strategic in nature and only a few understand the value of, or the approach to, strategic communication.

This section will focus on implementing a strategic communication effort for your organization--something you must have regardless of the size or net worth of the business. It will discuss various ways to improve internal and external communication. Lack of effective communication within an organization is a sure way to build the walls around the silos that already exist. Externally, ineffective communication with the customer creates a different type of silo that makes the company "out-of-touch" with this most important person to the business.

The key aspect of strategic communication for an organization is the development and implementation of a strategic communication plan that aligns with the organization's strategy. The problem is, many people do not understand what a strategic communication plan is--it is not a plan to communicate the strategic plan and it is not a marketing strategy (these are subsets of strategic communication). In fact, most companies do not even have a strategic communication plan or, if they have one, a team to manage it.

A strategic communication plan is fully aligned to the organization's strategic plan (i.e., it should be developed to further the mission and vision of the organization). The strategic communication plan should contain six things:

- ▸ Themes
- ▸ Key Messages
- ▸ Audience Groups
- ▸ Communication Tools
- ▸ Communication Strategy
- ▸ Communication Performance Measurement

The purpose of this type of plan is to: 1) Organize all organizational communication around themes and key messages targeted to specific audience groups; 2) Improve internal and external communication through specific strategic communications activities; 3) Measure communication success; and 4) Continually improve communicative effectiveness.

Understanding that strategic communication could be an entire book unto itself, we will provide only a basic understanding of the concepts behind a strategic communication plan. The key word in the title is "strategic." A strategic communication plan aligns first and foremost to the strategic plan. Like the information technology strategy (see next section below), this is an important subordinate plan to any strategic organization.

The best plans are built starting with a purpose and way to measure their effectiveness. Then, the organization determines its audience groups, conducts an audience analysis, and develops the themes and key messages. After this, a tool inventory is completed, and communication strategies are developed, implemented, and measured according to the plan. The major elements of a strategic communication plan are described as follows:

1. **Themes**: Themes in a communication plan are like goals to a strategic plan. These are very broad conceptual messages that the organization focuses its communication efforts around.

   For example, a Theme might be, *"Myopia.org strives to fulfill customers' needs at the lowest costs possible."*

2. **Key Messages**: Once the themes are defined and understood, key messages that align to these identified themes are developed. It is best to use a modified mind mapping technique to determine and align key messages.

   For example, three Key Messages for Myopia.org's theme, "**Myopia.org strives to fulfill customers' needs at the lowest costs possible**," might be:

   - *Myopia.org's Strategic Plan emphasizes fulfilling customers' needs at the lowest costs possible as a strategic imperative.*

- *Myopia.org applies continuous process improvement to ensure it is meeting its customers' needs at the lowest costs possible.*
- *Myopia.org focuses on balanced budgeting and keeping resource costs in check to ensure customers' costs are controlled.*

3. **Audience Groups**: Using interviews and brainstorming, the organization determines who the audience members are--both internally and externally. Remember that a strategic communication plan is directed at internal and external communication--both of which are crucial. Once you know who your communication customers (audience) are, you need to analyze what they know, what they do not know, what you want them to know, and how they prefer to receive the message. This is referred to as an audience analysis.

An effective and repeatable way to analyze your audience is with the communication continuum. This is a measurement assessment that the organization conducts based off both its assessment and its understanding. This chart plots audience members along the continuum of awareness, understanding, acceptance, and advocacy (*shown in Figure 7*). Once you know your audience members through your completed assessment, group the audience members based on where they are on the continuum and what they need to know. This will allow you to align key messages to these groups versus trying to speak to each audience member differently.

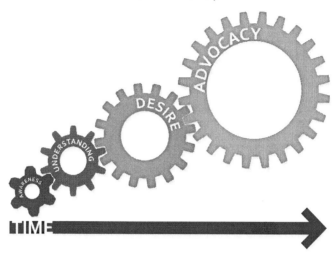

Figure 7: Communication Continuum

4. **Communication Tools**: When you conduct your audience analysis, audience members will identify how they prefer to receive the communication message. Internally, the organization should take an inventory of all the communication tools it currently uses (e.g., email, magazine, television, social media, etc.). Based on these two items, you can address any organizational gaps in communication methods (tools) and build them into your strategy (see below).

For instance, perhaps several of Myopia.org's external audience members are active on LinkedIn and are avid blog readers on the site, but the company does not have a presence on LinkedIn, let alone post and blog there. This absence easily identifies a significant communication tool gap that they need to close.

5. **Communication Strategy**: The communication strategy outlines the objectives of the strategic communication plan that align to the organization's strategic plan and supports the rest of the strategic communication plan. Simply put, these are the three to five-year actions to be taken to improve communication strategically within the organization. This section of the plan will contain the specific actions required as well as a table that aligns themes, key messages, and tools to target key audience groups.

   An example of a strategic action for Myopia.org might be, *"To develop, implement, and measure a robust social media communication program that involves: Facebook, Twitter, and LinkedIn; participation in key discussion groups; daily updates to the social media platforms; and weekly blogging."*

6. **Communication Performance Measurement**: Plans are just "shelfware" if you do not measure their effectiveness after implementation, provide accountability, and allow for adjustment when original actions are not working. You must first determine the purposes of your strategic communication plan, so you can measure its eventual effectiveness.

For example, let us say that Myopia.org has a less than favorable customer opinion and it aligns one of the purposes in its plan to *improve customer opinion*. Now, it has focused its communication on the outcome. Sure, it is important to measure activities, like the number of blog posts each week or number of website hits, but the true measurement focus should be on the expected results of those measures. You can blog all day and not change someone's opinion or even get someone to read your blogs. The plan must measure the implementation of the action items against expectations. As described above in Section 3, accountability to the measurement plan is key, and sometimes the authority needs to reside with a specific organization or entity.

In summary, the strategic communication plan should focus internally and externally and be strategic in nature. Tactical plans, like subordinate communication plans and marketing plans, exist under the umbrella of the strategic communication plan. Let us now discuss the different characteristics of internal and external focus.

Internal focus. Even organizations that have a strong communications program often fail to focus on the most important aspect--internal communication. Themes and key messages need to target the internal customers and stakeholders (headquarters, leaders, managers, employees, and even employees' families) as well as the external customers and stakeholders. Internal communication messages and tools can be completely different than external (e.g., an organizational town hall to highlight the employee impact of an organizational change).

Operational collaboration is also an important aspect of internal and, sometimes, external communication. An organization should examine and work to improve the tools associated with collaboration on its work projects. Some examples of this type of open collaboration could be: development and improvement of knowledge management tools that allow for electronic collaboration such as SharePoint® Team Sites and Wikis; regular operational meetings that are focused on key organizational end-to-end processes; leadership and recognition newsletters focused on internal operational activities; and transparency of performance measurement data across the organization to all levels. Tools, like Skype® and Slack®, should be used to improve virtual collaboration.

Personal and professional communication within an organization can be important to employee development and engagement. Using forums and groups, either formally or informally, in-person or online, can be effective. Myopia.org, has sales members spread out across all the operational teams who reach back to tools in the Finance Branch. Developing a monthly forum to discuss key changes to finance processes and tools as well as successes in the financial sales community ensures everyone is on the same sheet of music. Couple that with an online sales community on the company intranet and you have an effective tool for both new and seasoned sales professionals.

Employee satisfaction and engagement should be measured every year, at a minimum, to determine gaps and to develop strategic, operational, and tactical plans to improve. Leaders should not focus their efforts on simply improving the scores on their satisfaction and engagement surveys, but should focus on doing the right things that result in improved results. Although employee engagement aligns many things, it is a key aspect of your internal communication activities and should feed your annual assessment. The number one problem with employee engagement is a lack of communication!

External focus. Close to 100% of all customer-facing organizations have some type of external communication approach. Only about 20% of these approaches are ever fully developed. Essentially, 80% of all customer communication fails to achieve any specifically desired result. Essentially, most of the time your external communication is just noise-- now you know why people tune out commercials and throw away advertisements in the mail. We are being programed, as a culture, to ignore communications because most of them are worthless to us.

Successful companies understand their audience, develop themes and key messages, deliver the message consistently to meet customers' needs, and measure the results of their messages. For those that do not, this section was written for you--you are siloed from your customer.

Traditional communication methods have been around for decades. These are things like television, magazines, newspapers, fliers, and mass mailing. Understanding that most of this type of communication is filtered right into our mental and physical trash receptacles, makes this a very difficult media to be successful in. Thus, we must focus on being more personal in our communication activities when using traditional means. Repeating a phone number three times in an ad might statistically get more phone calls, but it does not guarantee an expected result. Aligning our traditional message to the specific needs of our audience is bound to result in fewer calls, but better results. For this reason, organizations are increasingly moving to content marketing over traditional marketing activities.

Social media is also becoming the new frontier for external communication for many organizations. With this category, we also include the more traditional web presence, because the goal of social media should be to replicate the Internet message and drive customers to that web presence for more information. Building a Facebook page and saying that "we're using social media," is like riding a bike without tires-- it will get you nowhere. If your company determines that the audience is savvy to an Internet and social media world, then by all means pursue social media and the Internet, but do it with purpose.

Social media communication must be constant, responsive, and controlled. This means that you must be constantly communicating (almost daily, but not more than once per day) about things that are important to the audience groups you want to affect. This also means that activities that surround your social media postings, like comments, re-blog-ging/re-tweeting, etc. reinforce your action and purpose.

Offensive materials posted to your social media platforms should be removed from the public eye, but feedback (regardless of how bad it is) that is honestly posted should not be filtered. Nothing is worse than removing a negative comment on your post or site because it makes you look bad. The person who put it there knows you removed it. How does that affect your reputation? However, this does not apply to someone's comment that excessively blasts you on the Internet to defame or belittle you.

Non-traditional forms of communication can also be used. They include some of the more inventive ways of sharing your message, such as: trade shows, conferences, blogging, podcasting, and online radio. Consider that one of the key techniques in self-publishing these days is to give away free books for several days or give away a certain number of books so that more people will read and comment on your book, thus increasing its exposure in the search engine ratings. Thus, giving away free books often results in more people purchasing the book. Organizations should explore these non-traditional methods to drive their key messages to their audience groups.

Customer satisfaction and engagement measurements, like for employees, should be collected at least on an annual basis through recurring surveys. The results of the surveys can then feed the communications strategy and help to determine the effectiveness of both communications and operations. This information feeds future audience analysis activities and leads to a better strategic communication plan year-over-year.

Change Communication. Change communication is a cross category affecting internal and, sometimes, external communication. When an organization starts to consider conducting any change (i.e., strategic, organizational, process, program, product, etc.) it should also consider how it will communicate the change before, during, and after it has occurred. For every major change your organization engages in, it should consider utilizing change communication. Small changes often just need a little thought, while others might require a full-blown change communication plan. Regardless of the magnitude of the change, change communication is important and can facilitate success of the change effort.

Communication is such a major concern in almost every organization. Mainly because it is happening without the benefit of any strategic thought. To break through the silos and OM in your organization, you need to get smarter about communicating strategically both internally and externally.

Remember that everything outlined in this book is focused on changing the way things are today and while you change, you must communicate the changes well.

After careful consultation between Kevin and John, Myopia.org embarked on the development of a strategic communication plan to accompany its newly created strategic plan. One of the first things Kevin did was establish a two-person Communication Branch under the Support Division and hire two communication experts to staff it. They were directed to work with John and Dana to develop and implement a strategic communication plan for Myopia.org. Within a few months, communication across Myopia.org, both internally and externally, improved considerably through their tactical efforts. The leadership team approved the new plan to improve communications and implementation began in earnest.

Additionally, as part of the communications plan, the two-person communications team partnered with Dana to design professional development classes for leadership and management. These classes focused on strategy, management, and communication on topics designed to improve the skills of the staff. Myopia.org used the training programs to expand the staff's knowledge of its strategic plans and direction. This was an excellent way for the teams to conduct change communication around their respective plans.

In one short year, Myopia.org was well on its way to becoming a more effective communicative organization and its next annual assessment proved just that to the leadership team.

Section 9
Integrated Operations Means Integrated Information Management

Kevin scratched his head and muttered to himself as he pored over a recent report received from the Information Technology Panel within Myopia.org's Corporate Governance structure.

In reviewing processes, the panel determined that many of their information technology systems did not communicate with each other. There was an apparent "invisible firewall" between the Operations and Support Division and, in Operations, which had replicated databases and spreadsheets -- sometimes down to the individual -- to manage work. This information technology redundancy cost Myopia.org an estimated $30M over the last ten years in development and maintenance. This situation also caused a great deal of communication and collaboration issues across the organization.

Additionally, the report highlighted that the Information Branch Chief's introverted nature resulted in his organizational involvement mainly as a "help desk." He refused to do anything broad across the agency. Because of his inaction, the panel recommended a thorough review of the entire information structure within Myopia.org; development of an enterprise information technology strategy; and movement towards better integration and control.

Bill's stance on this was that, not only was he understaffed to manage a study of this magnitude, but it would undoubtedly fail because all attempts in the past to integrate information systems had failed.

It is crucial to understand your end-to-end processes, as highlighted earlier in this book. That understanding will enable you to break through the silos that form within your organization. In many ways, though, truly efficient processes are often hampered by an inability of information systems to "communicate" with one another.

The silos within the information technology areas of an organization are often buried deep and frequently go undetected. This occurs because of a lack of integrated and interoperable systems and operations.

Below are some of the root causes we previously discussed that are associated with OM in the area of information technology:

1. **Strategy:** An organization that lacks an effective long-term, strategic focus often fails to think about big-picture integration and interoperability of information systems. Once an organization begins thinking about how it will achieve its vision, it often finds out that its information technology systems do not operate effectively and efficiently enough to support that vision. With systems work, "strategy" is seldom more than 18-months-out and focuses mainly on break-fix and compliance requirements--essentially a "help desk" mentality.

2. **Accountability:** It is crucial to have common measures across the organization in order to be able to gauge its progress towards a specific point in the

future. However, real-time visibility of these measures in a dashboard framework that allows for roll up to the highest level; drill down to the individual process; and alignment to the strategic plan is crucial. Information technology forms the backbone of this type of dashboard. The dashboard must have the ability to pull information from the systems versus requiring re-entry of information. Systems that need re-entry require a great deal of effort; create errors in reporting; and prevent the capability of real-time reporting. Additionally, the dashboard systems should provide the capability for current state and future possibility analysis. Businesses need this type of data at their fingertips and everyone in the organization needs to know how this information relates to the strategy, so they know how they support and impact the mission and vision.

3. **Organization:** Organizational structure, in itself, creates information silos. Review the various information solutions already created across your organization through stand-alone databases and spreadsheets. Then create one enterprise-wide solution that is interoperable with other systems, like human resources and operations, and meets all groups' needs. This is especially helpful in bringing organizations into a matrixed structure because the systems improve the ability of these structures to operate and communicate.

4. **Process:** End-to-end processes seldom exist within one single software system and, in many ways, it is

impossible to orient all the information tools required into one system. Bringing them together through an integrated and interoperable approach can greatly improve the end-to-end process.

When conducting process improvement, emphasize leaning out the physical process first before leaping to automation of that process. Automation can bring an improvement in process efficiency, but failing to create a lean, repeatable process before automation can significantly impact the effectiveness of the process. Focus on a staged "crawl, walk, run" approach to process improvement:

- o Crawl: Improve the physical process so that you have removed as much of the special cause variance as possible making it a standardized process.
- o Walk: Develop simple data capture (e.g., spreadsheets and databases) and software-enabled processes (e.g., using email, SharePoint®, or Salesforce® to manage workload) that work with the new leaned process.
- o Run: Develop an IT-supported interoperable information system solution that automates the improved process.

5. **Resources:** Information systems (hardware and software) are normally a major player within the ongoing battle for corporate resources. Although these systems are usually budgeted differently than salary, general, and administrative expenses, the cost to

make a significant software upgrade can be staggering because most or all systems must be brought to the same level at once. Limited licenses may fix immediate problems but deny the organization the enterprise-wide capability of key software. Having parts of your organization on different versions of a productivity system, like email, can significantly impact efficiency and effectiveness of. Additionally, decisions not to upgrade hardware equally across an organization can negatively impact enterprise-wide software updates and capabilities.

Although hardware and software normally fall low in the resource battle, when it is needed, its need becomes undeniably critical. Another information system resource constraint--lack of information system programmers, developers, and support to build and maintain systems required to meet the demand--needs to be considered. Planning for these resource constraints is crucial for an organization to deal with siloes of information.

Integrated versus Interoperable. The primary cause of information technology silos in an organization is the inability of information systems to talk to each other and/or work together. What this creates is a redundancy of systems that cascades to a redundancy of data across the organization. The larger and more fractured an organization becomes, the more prevalent and invasive this issue becomes.

Organizations have traditionally moved to become more "integrated" with their systems. What does that mean and what is the difference between "integrated" and "interoperable?" The goal is to break through the silos created by information systems that fail to talk and work together. First, let us examine the definitions of integrated and interoperable:

Integrated: The act of forming, coordinating, or blending into a functioning or unified whole. Integration allows data from one device or software to be read or manipulated by another, resulting in ease of use.

Interoperable: The ability of two or more systems or components to exchange information and to use the information that has been exchanged. Interoperable systems possess the capability to exchange data via a common set of business procedures, and to read and write the same file formats and use the same protocols.

Both types describe interactions between core separate systems. The difference is how they work together. Integrated systems communicate through the use of special codes created to transfer information back and forth. You may have seen systems where you pull data through a regular (e.g., nightly) batch operation and enter that data into another system. This is usually done by pulling from one set of tables into another set of tables through a separate routine that tells each system which table cell equates to which table cell. The best way to think about this is as a language translator.

Interoperable means that two or more systems remain unchanged and the systems work together even though they were not necessarily designed to work together when built. Integrating two (or more) systems through custom code that are already interoperable is trivial; you just have to configure them to work together. Integrating non-interoperable systems takes much more work. The beauty of interoperability is that two systems developed completely independently can still work together. This is done by following a set of standards (or at least specifications) that agree on the same description language and protocols.

To integrate or to interoperate...that is the question. Regardless of the approach your organization decides to employ, and how mature (see Capability Maturity Model below) you desire your information technology to be, the important goal is to reduce the redundancy of systems and data instances across the company. The larger an organization, the more difficult this is to get a handle on, much less accomplish. Much like process improvement, the steps are:

1. Define the as-is, high-level systems architecture for the organization.
2. Catalog all major and minor systems across the organization, making sure you track the versions and types, as these often vary.
3. Define the to-be systems architecture that meets the strategic vision of the organization.
4. Develop an information technology strategy that works in line with the organization's strategic plan.

5. Implement.

Capability Maturity Model. In 1988, Watts Humphrey from Carnegie Mellon University created an effective methodology to evaluate programs and systems using a five-stage measurement system. This approach was referred to as the Capability Maturity Model. Since the development of the first model, it has been used by many organizations to effectively evaluate different types of technology systems.

The Capability Maturity Model Integration (CMMI) was later developed to evaluate multiple information technology systems within and across an organization. CMMI is an information technology approach to measure the maturity of an entire technology program and can provide several benefits to any organizations. CMMI provides the following benefits:

▸ A place for the organization to start improving its program
▸ Considers the organization's prior experiences to get to where it is today
▸ Provides a common language and a shared vision across the organization and among the information technology community
▸ Outlines a specific framework for identifying and prioritizing step-by-step actions
▸ Clearly defines what improvement means for your organization
▸ Allows for a benchmark for comparative assessment of your organization against various other organizations

Technology silos represent silos within silos within silos. They are sometimes so hidden, that we do not even realize they exist. However, they significantly impact an organization's ability to serve its mission and purpose. These silos must be identified and minimized through integration and interoperability to be built using a capability maturity roadmap.

Kevin, Stan, Bill, Dana, and John met over several weeks to gather information, discuss the current situation, and consider future strategies. Eventually, Bill's team was able to break out of its old way of thinking and become more strategic. For the first year and half, it had a rough road and Kevin had to redirect funds toward additional strategic support for the Information Branch. Ultimately, an Information Systems Governance Working Group, under Myopia.org's governance structure, presented a strategic and unified information technology multi-year plan designed to redefine Myopia.org as an automation-enabled business.

Kevin returned from a recent meeting with his superiors where he presented the one-year report card from their capability maturity model along with the five-year strategy for Myopia.org. Bill was promoted to chief information officer for Myopia.org's parent organization. The entire Information Branch staff and the Information Systems Governance Working Group was recognized inside the organization and by several external publications for their efforts and accomplishments.

Part 5
Conclusion

Every organization--everyone in fact--potentially suffers from issues related to Organizational Myopia (OM). You cannot break down the silos to fix these problems--that only creates a bigger problem. Understand that the forming of OM results from a human tendency consequent to the natural transition of growth for an organization. You can overcome it by successfully evaluating the nine areas outlined in this book and dealing with those as desired. This can result in years of work for an organization to truly eliminate OM, but it must preserve as it can easily slip back into OM if its focus wanes. It is not required to have someone like John come in and point out these areas, but professional expertise can always be helpful to identify and solve issues. However, regardless of how OM is identified, the organization has to "own" the problem and "work" to fix it.

Hopefully, this book has helped you better identify your own OM issues and provided significant ideas for overcoming OM wherever it strikes. Keep this reference on hand as you move through your strategic journey and share it with your leadership and management teams--this should be required reading for everyone in your organization.

If you have learned anything from this book, it should be that silos always exist, and you actually want them as your organization grows--in fact, you need them. What you do not need is for these silos to start driving a myopic view of how the organization runs.

Everyone will tell you that silos are bad and that they need to be broken down or removed. Thus, we spend all our time trying to break down the silos, when we should be breaking *through* them and getting to the root causes of OM.

You cannot fight human nature and our inherent need to form into groups. Plus, silos allow us to focus efforts, they instill healthy competition, and they facilitate organizational operations. Destroying them for the sake of improvement never works.

OM can be overcome with the systematic application of a full-spectrum of strategic and organizational improvement methods. Organizations need to understand the concerns and emphasis of both leadership and employees and, then, identify and tackle the root causes in a methodical manner.

The nine areas we discussed in Part Four of this book are summarized here:

Leadership Development: Leadership enlightenment and development is the first step to eliminating OM from your organization. Just sharing this book with all the leaders in your organization will do wonders for improvement. Understanding why silos exist, how to look for the root causes of OM, and what to do about these things is a crucial first step.

Strategy and Vision: Organizations and employees need solid and inspiring direction to be effective. If your strategy does not make sense, or is not properly resourced, everyone will struggle to understand it and achieve it. Unfortunately, 70% of all strategies fail to achieve what they set out to accomplish. When done right, strategic planning is effective in providing sound improvement and eliminating OM.

Accountability: Performance measurement, aligned to the organization's strategy, is critical to organizational success. The best approach to creating accountability is to formalize your performance management program with a plan of action and assigned resources to drive the effort. Otherwise, measures themselves can conflict and create their own type of silos.

Culture: Organizational culture, and microcultures, in your organization exist. They form invisible silos that breed OM. Changing the culture of an organization is tremendously difficult--it takes time and effort. However, with proper effort and analysis, organizational cultures can be changed through behavioral tactics.

Reorganization and Governance: One of the most important lessons in this book is to stop breaking down the silos to fix OM in your organization. If organization, itself, is part of your OM problem, then start with corporate governance efforts. Sometimes an organizational restructure is required, but it should be done correctly and for the right reasons.

Cross-functionality and Customer Focus: Once you start to fully understand who your true customers are, and what it is you deliver, you start breaking through process silos through end-to-end processes. Tools, such as value chain analysis, SIPOCs, and a process catalog help to focus the entire organization. This leads to a culture of continuous improvement that engages all employees in day-to-day business improvement and eliminates OM.

Resource Distribution: The biggest wall builder, when it comes to silos and OM, is allocation of resources. Someone always has more than you and you never have enough. A fair, equitable, and transparent resource determination and allocation approach is key to overcoming OM.

Communication: Insufficient or inadequate communication is one of the biggest problems in any organization. It is always a challenge to communicate effectively. It is not that communication is not occurring, but that it occurs without strategic thought. Externally and internally, organizations must get better at understanding and implementing strategic communication. This is a critical element to overcoming OM.

Integrated Operations: The last section we covered was the technology silo. Technology that is not integrated or interoperable creates islands of operation, or technology silos. Organizations should aggressively identify and break through these silos using a capability maturity roadmap.

OM in your organization has probably built itself up over years. It has embedded itself in every facet of your organization, from leadership, to technology, and everywhere in between. Solving the issues related to this OM will not be easy. This book was designed to formulate a roadmap for diagnosing and solving problems related to silos in your organization which lead to the formation of OM. Good luck in overcoming your OM!

ABOUT THE AUTHOR

John Knotts is a strategic business advisor with over 25 years of experience in military, non-profit, and commercial leadership and consulting. He has an extensive background in strategy, change, process, leadership, management, human capital, training and education, innovation, design, and communication. He believes strongly in a holistic and nononsense approach to establishing operational excellence.

A 21-year Air Force Veteran and former consultant with the top-rated consulting firm, Booz | Allen | Hamilton, John recently held several strategic roles with the United Services Automobile Association (USAA). John also owns his own consulting business, Crosscutter Enterprises, with which he has sharpened the saw since retiring from the Air Force in 2008. He has been very involved in several non-profit organizations since the early 1990s.

John is currently a Doctoral student in the field of Industrial and Organizational Psychology. He holds a Master's Degree in Quality Systems Management from National Graduate

School and his Bachelor's is in Management from American Military School. He has a Lean Six Sigma Master Black Belt from Smarter Solutions, a Master's-level certification as a Change Management Advanced Practitioner from Georgetown University, and Change Management certification from Prosci. Additionally, he has had extensive training and education in Information Technology Infrastructure Library (ITIL), project management, and agile methodologies.

John boasts an extensive writing, speaking, facilitating, and teaching background. In the Air Force, he was instructor certified, and taught hundreds of classes in many areas. He is an Advanced Toastmaster with experience in ten different clubs in Europe and the United States. John is also a certified Master Speechwriter, studying under Joan Detz, professional speechwriter and coach. As a Master Black Belt, he has developed and conducted numerous process improvement and process management courses. For both National Graduate School and Hallmark University, John has been an Adjunct Faculty member. John previously published a fictional novel, **One Dead Marine**, and has also been an avid blogger.

John and his wife, Lori, enjoy horses, golf, reading, writing, and traveling. Together, they own Fine Print Farms, an Equestrian Eventing Destination in the Texas Hill Country. They also are the founders of two equine-related non-profits. The first is Hill Country Eventing Foundation, designed to support and promote the equestrian sport of Eventing in the Texas Hill Country and South Texas. The second, a passion of Lori and John's, is Reckless Rangers Veteran's Equitherapy.

Through this program, they provide free equine-based learning and therapy to veterans dealing with post-traumatic stress.

John invites you to Connect with and Follow him and his business endeavors, through social media platforms such as:

- ▸ LinkedIn: www.linkedin.com/in/johnknotts77
- ▸ Facebook: www.facebook.com/john.knotts1
- ▸ Twitter: www.twitter.com/johnrknotts/

Interested in further discussing this topic with John? Want him to come to your organization? Looking for a speaker with lots to share? Email John today at John.Knotts@crossctr.com and let him know how he can help.

GET THE ROADMAP WORKBOOK *(COMING SOON)*

Love the book? Interested in applying the sections outlined in the nine areas, but not sure where to start? What if you had an assessment tool that helped you pinpoint potential OM-related problems in your organization and then provided you with the ability to plan out how to overcome them?

This spiral-bound roadmap workbook walks you through diagnosing your organizational myopia, identifies what to work on in what order, and provides tools, tips, and tricks, to overcome OM in your organization.

This roadmap workbook will only available by special order.

Pre-order your
Overcoming Organizational Myopia Roadmap Workbook
today!

Place your order at
https://johnknotts-author.com

With this pre-order opportunity, each roadmap workbook is $149.99 (savings of $100 off the full $249.99 retail price) -- bulk order prices also available -- and chock full of helpful resources. Starting with a fully-comprehensive assessment tool, this roadmap workbook guides you step-by-step as if you were working with a highly-paid consulting team. Each problem has specific tools, tips, and tricks aligned to facilitate solving it.

RELATED WORKS BY JOHN KNOTTS

Overcoming Organizational Myopia is John's initial work, highlighting his many areas of expertise he has utilized to break through siloed organizations. This book forms the initial platform for several future business titles that will be related to the nine areas addressed in it.

Sign up at John's author site, https://johnknotts-author.com, to watch for these 16 future titles to be released, and keep in touch as new titles appear.

- *Leaderment® and Leader Youniversity®*
- *Corporate Epidemic: Toxic Leadership and Undead Businesses*
- *Getting Ahead in the Corporate World*
- *Choices We Have--Decisions We Make*
- *Think Big Take Small Steps*
- *Becoming A High Performing Organization*
- *Organizational Commitment: Your Employees Can Be Heroes Too*
- *Employee Engagement in Four Steps*
- *Stop Jumping To Do: A PDCA Approach to Project Planning and Problem Solving*
- *Building a Culture of Continuous Improvement*
- *Getting Good @ Process Improvement*
- *Experience-based Operational Excellence*
- *Breaking the Intelligent Automation Paradigm*
- *Ready...Set...Change: Change Management is Dead, Long Live Change Readiness!*
- *Maturing Your Document Domain*
- *A Formula for Innovation*

Leadership Development

Leaderment® and *Leader Youniversity®*

True Leadership is a dying art. The great leaders of the past, George Washington, Winston Churchill, Alexander the Great, Martin Luther King, even Adolph Hitler, are now few-and-far between. Some successful leaders, such as Steve Jobs, have risen to an iconic status. But have they been truly great leaders or were they just successful at running something?

Often, the skills a leader needs are inconsistent with those needed by a manager. I believe that if you are not a good leader, you will also not be a good manager, and, if you are not a good manager, you will also not be a good leader. It is my contention that those who apply both talents expertly demonstrate what I call, "Leaderment." This is the expert combination of the skills required for Leadership and Management.

Leaderment is a master-planned series of six volumes that culminate in a certification from the Leader Youniversity. This certification program is comprised of a set of five workbooks; each containing specific tools designed to improve your leadership and management skills.

Leaderment: Becoming A Better Leader and Manager, will be available through traditional book channels (printed and eBook). The five Leaderment workbooks, are part of the Leader Youniversity and will only be available upon registration for completion of the leadership certification program.

Leadership Development

Corporate Epidemic: Toxic Leadership and Undead Businesses

Bad Leadership is Becoming an Epidemic!

Everywhere I look, I see evidence of bad leadership. The most prevalent problems are leadership apathy and leaders that lack accountability, the "it's good enough" leaders and the leaders who are "just getting by."

"Why are we seeing this," you ask yourself?

Bad leaders hire and promote bad people. And, unfortunately, bad leadership is not just destroying corporate America, but it is doing it at a record pace; the effects of which, will extend far into the future.

These leadership charlatans are building armies of apathy whose members will follow in their footsteps. If you are someone who gets things done, you are kept in a position to get things done because bad leaders do not want you in a leadership position--you threaten them!

No wonder more than 70% of employees are disengaged at work. Who would not be with such a depressing and disheartening leadership outlook? Do you really have to be lazy and barely competent to get ahead?

Bad leaders are running rampant in corporate America and the undead companies they lead are foundering. Is there nothing that can be done?

Leadership Development

Getting Ahead in the Corporate World

Getting ahead in the corporate world is like driving. There are five types of drivers on a multi-lane business highway:

The first type of driver is the slow poke who picks a lane and drives under the speed limit. This type is happy not getting ahead fast.

The second, is the one who always takes the fast lane and stays there, riding the tail of the person in front of them, hoping that person will move over or go faster. Someone else going even faster always ends up in that lane and eventually comes up to ride the second driver's tail.

The third type of driver thinks the road was put there just for them. They use every lane on their commute, travelling as fast as they can. They are dangerous, and they switch lanes often, cutting others off.

Then, there is the risk taker type of driver, who sees the traffic and gets off the highway onto side streets, hoping to pass that traffic and re-enter ahead of others.

The last type is the methodical driver. These people stay at a safe speed limit for the road conditions, travel in the slower lanes, only pass when necessary, plan their routes, and are ready for the trip's end well in advance.

What type of driver are you?

Leadership Development

Choices We Have--Decisions We Make

Every day--at work and at home--we are faced with choices. Some of these choices are actually big decisions, while others are as simple as, "Do I want fries with that, or do I want a salad?" Have you ever stopped to consider the variety of options you need to respond to and how your response to these options is formulated?

Sometimes, we simply jump to our decisions--we do not look before we leap. At those times, it is not until after making the decision that we really examine the choices we had and the ramifications of our decision.

We are, ultimately, faced with three possible decisions to the choices presented to us. Sometimes, following the decision we make for one choice, we have to then make another decision based upon that first decision, and so on. The decisions to each choice are, Easy, Normal, and Hard.

Our lives are made up of choices and decisions. Simple things such as: should we eat fast food, which is cheap and easy, but tends to be bad for us; do we eat at a nice restaurant, which generally has better choices and food, but costs more; or do we take the time and effort to purchase food at a grocery store or other outlet, where we get more for our money, but then must prepare the food, which takes time and effort are choices we are faced with daily.

We are faced with hundreds of these decisions throughout the day and make decisions without putting much thought into the choices available to us. Making better, more informed decisions – in our daily lives and in our business lives – can be done through the use of a simple approach outlined in this book.

Strategy and Vision
Think Big Take Small Steps

Proper Strategic Planning is the Most Important First Step for Any Organization.

FORTUNE Magazine, in 1999, published the article "Why CEOs Fail," which stated, "70% of all strategies fail to achieve their desired results and 30% fail to achieve anything at all." Planning, specifically strategic planning, tends to fail for many reasons. These reasons can be grouped into five specific categories that can be placed into a structured and systematic process of planning to ensure success. They are:

▶ Executable Focus
▶ Strategic Framework
▶ Traceable Implementation
▶ Rigor and Accountability
▶ Communication

Leadership must own this process. If leadership passes this strategic planning initiative over to others, even if they satisfy all five categories during their strategic planning activities, the organization's planning will always fail.

Think Big, Take Small Steps is a no-nonsense strategic planning guide that takes away the mysticism and confusion surrounding strategic planning and breaks the planning process down into three simple and easy to follow phases that include those five categories. This book demonstrates how to create winning strategies and turn them into executable and trackable strategic plans.

Strategy and Vision
Becoming A High Performing Organization

Over the years, I have worked with many businesses--nonprofits, government, and corporations. Many organizations ascribe to the statement made by Voltaire, "Perfect is the enemy of good." What Voltaire is saying is that achieving absolute perfection becomes increasingly inefficient because the increasing effort results in diminishing returns. Essentially, good is good enough. This is something I am simply not able to believe.

Every organization can become a high performing organization. The common belief in business is that there is a finite pie and each company fights for a piece of this pie. I believe that the existence of the pie is a falsehood. If you are a high performing organization, and deliver goods and services in a quality manner, worrying about your "piece of the pie" is a waste of time and energy. To succeed, do not focus on this nonexistent "pie", rather, focus on being the best you can be.

The problem is, organizations simply do not know how to become high performing. There are slews of books and research on the subject, but somehow, how to actually become high performing often alludes organizations. Perhaps, it is because they choose to believe Voltaire and the countless others who caution against setting goals too high and they hold everyone back in the belief that achieving your best simply is just too hard or even unattainable.

Becoming a High Performing Organization provides you with the tools to put all that nonsense behind you. This work and, its associated products, are designed to eradicate the myths that hold organizations back with easy-to-follow formulas to become the high performing organization you desire.

Culture

Organizational Commitment: Your Employees Can Be Heroes Too

There is a fable about a chicken, a pig, and breakfast. The fable says the chicken is fully dedicated to providing breakfast because she works hard to provide the eggs. The pig; however, is fully committed to providing breakfast because he gives his life to provide the bacon. In a sense, the pig is breakfast's hero, sacrificing his life for the mission--the ultimate in organizational commitment.

Research on organizational commitment often describes it as, "The employee's psychological attachment to the organization." The works of Meyer and Allen segregate organizational commitment into three components--affective, continuance, and normative. In *The Art of Winning Commitment*, Dick Richards states that there are four forms of commitment: 1) Political, 2) Intellectual, 3) Emotional, and 4) Spiritual.

Although the definitions categorize the concept of organizational commitment, they do little to explain what this type of commitment really is. In fact, there is little established work that pinpoints what organizational commitment actually is, or more importantly, how to cultivate it in the workplace. In other words, these definitions are incomplete and flawed.

In *Organizational Commitment,* we develop a new definition, consisting of a demonstration of dedication, loyalty, and sacrifice to an organization. It is the demonstration of these three basic tenants, regardless of the organization's type, that constitutes organizational commitment. By understanding and applying this new definition, you can learn how help your employees become fully committed heroes.

Culture

Employee Engagement in Four Steps

For the last ten years, businesses have focused on employee engagement and the cost associated with a lack of engagement to businesses. Virtually any report or study on engagement points out that about 70% of employees in the U.S. are not engaged at work and that is costing businesses approximately $500 billion a year.

Although the nomenclature is different, this employee-focused issue has not really changed since before the 1950s when the emphasis was on employee satisfaction. In the 1980s, the emphasis turned to organizational commitment. Regardless of what it is called, the same business issue has not changed since researchers started studying and quantifying it more than 70 years ago.

Engagement is the term that confuses managers the most. What is being measured is how employees feel about their jobs. This is difficult for companies to manage to. So, they do what they think will work and manage to single items that received low scores on an engagement survey.

Employees are, essentially, engaged by four things at work: organization; communication; development; and quality. For some reason, it is not obvious to organizations that this is where employees' focus lies. Thus, these four things become some of the major problem areas in many companies.

Employee Engagement in Four Steps covers these in depth in order to help any organization understand and improve its employee engagement.

Cross-functionality and Customer Focus

Stop Jumping To Do: A PDCA Approach to Project Planning and Problem Solving

We are faced with a task...

Our boss says one of these things to us: "I need 'x' done."; "Our product is not selling as well as we expected."; "In our annual strategy meeting we were assigned a strategic objective."; or "Something is wrong in our process and we are really not sure why."

Every day, millions and millions of people around the world are facing a task--something that needs to get done. This usually takes the form of a project or problem to be solved.

It is in our human nature to solve problems. We jump right in and do the thing we are tasked with; or fix the problem. However, all too often, the work we do fails to achieve the objectives we set out to achieve. Why? Because we are "Jumping To Do."

It was several years ago that I stumbled upon a relatively simple, yet extremely effective, method I could use to implement any strategic plan. What I quickly realized was that this approach was the answer to any project-based challenge anyone is faced with today.

As stated, we want to solve problems, fix things, and implement projects. What I am going to provide to you in this book is a basic and simple planning tool that:

- ▶ Is easily repeatable
- ▶ Ensures project success
- ▶ Allows for simple timeline planning
- ▶ Takes less than an hour to complete

Cross-functionality and Customer Focus
Building a Culture of Continuous Improvement

A culture of continuous improvement provides any company a significant advantage in the marketplace. But do not take my word for it! An example is Corus, a customer focused, innovative solutions-driven company, which manufactures, processes and distributes steel and aluminum products and services to customers worldwide. Corus is already seeing the benefits of continuous improvement with:

- ▸ Reduced process waste
- ▸ Improved product quality
- ▸ Reduced re-work time
- ▸ Faster response times
- ▸ Driving costs down
- ▸ Retaining and gaining customers

Building a culture of continuous improvement is not easy and can take a considerable amount of time. However, it is achievable, and results will be felt within weeks, if not months, of seriously embarking on a journey to continuous improvement. Deciding to move toward a culture of continuous improvement, means becoming more strategic about how you manage your day-to-day operations. This is not about putting a few changes in place and calling it "good."

Over the past 25 plus years, I have developed a model for building this type of culture. This model centers on a strategy designed to build this type of culture in your organization. The strategy involves an equal portion of measuring, improving, and changing work. This model is fueled by a certain level of employee commitment and innovation. Learn about it in my upcoming book.

Cross-functionality and Customer Focus
Getting Good @ Process Improvement

Process improvement certification programs today have become watered down. People who receive a certification are educated just enough to pass. Organizations are filling up with employees with certifications. But are they really any good at process improvement and do these certifications even mean anything?

How Do You Get Really Good at Improving Processes?

Explore a multitude of ways to become better at improving processes in *Getting Good @ Process Improvement*. In this book, we will explore:

▸ External vs Internal and In-person vs Online
▸ With Project vs Without and Actual Project vs Simulation
▸ Formalized Training and Coaching vs Seat-of-your-Pants
▸ Testing vs No Testing
▸ Continuing Education Requirements
▸ Official Position vs Additional Duty
▸ Rely on Common Sense, Algebra, and Statistics
▸ Systems Thinking, Gap Analysis, and Bridge Building
▸ Being A Four-Year-Old--Asking Why
▸ Carrying a Big Toolbox
▸ Knowing the Difference Between Lean and Six Sigma
▸ Facilitation Like A Champ
▸ Thinking Like A Project Manager
▸ Alignment to Strategy
▸ Measure to Improve; the Measurement Cycle
▸ The Power of Go See and Digging Up Roots

Cross-functionality and Customer Focus
Experience-based Operational Excellence

An experience is a direct observation of, or participation in, events as a basis of knowledge. Experience occurs when an individual has been affected by, or gained knowledge through, direct observation of or participation in an event. Each individual's experience is filtered by his or her practical knowledge, skill, and training. Thus, two people can experience the same thing and have very different reactions.

Customer experience (CX) is something a customer personally encountered, experienced, or lived through with a certain company. It is the product of an interaction between a company and a customer over the duration of their relationship. This interaction includes the attraction, awareness, discovery, cultivation, and advocacy of the customer, and purchase and use of a service by that customer. This is what his or her opinion of the organization is based on.

Many companies today only focus on the "touchpoints"--the critical moments when customers interact with the company relative to its provision of a product or service to that customer to establish the customer experience. This is often depicted in marketing as an experience map. Customer experience is more than just touchpoints! All parts of an organization affect the customer. An emphasis on Operational Excellence within a company, as the driver of the customer experience, is important to carefully consider.

Cross-functionality and Customer Focus
Breaking the Intelligent Process Automation Paradigm

A process is nothing but a series of step-by-step tasks that begin with some type of request and end with the fulfillment of that request. Processes come in many shapes and sizes. The concepts of process management and process improvement have been around 100s of years.

Process automation in manufacturing began in the first Industrial Revolution. Intelligent Process Automation is a mindset and thought process of moving from a fully-manual process to a fully-automated solution.

This book outlines how to overcome the Five *Paradigms* of Intelligent Automation.

▸ Paradigm of the Shiny Object
▸ Paradigm of the Virtual Employee
▸ Paradigm of Done
▸ Paradigm of Tactical
▸ Paradigm of Ownership

Communication

Ready...Set...Change: Change Management is Dead, Long Live Change Readiness!

Since the 1940s, businesses have focused on change resistance and the management of change resistance. Companies and consultants are cashing in on the "Change Management" craze, but are we too late? Is that what we really ought to focus on? Change is constant and the speed of change is ever-increasing. Is it that we too late to manage change or is there simply too much change to manage?

In today's business world, if you are managing change, you are really too late. To be successful, businesses must be able to change quickly and change often. They need to be ready for change and view it as part of their daily existence.

Stop Managing Change
Start Building Change Readiness!

Ready...Set...Change talks about change, change management, and change readiness and takes the audience through the steps to become a Change Ready Business.

Integrated Operations
Maturing Your Document Domain

Document Management has become one of the most elusive business concerns of the information age. Businesses that aggressively seek to improve operations are now finding that they ignored their document production and management engine while they focused on improving products and services.

For many companies, the "document" has been looked at as a "necessary evil" and its development and delivery improvement has not kept up with improvements to the products or services. However, the number and size of documents are growing, and, for most companies, they are one of the most important assets a company has.

Many forward-thinking organizations make the mistake of believing that when they move to a digital platform, the "document" will go away. This is because, more-and-more, the physical document is being phased out for an electronic representation and organizations fail to understand that documents, tangible or not, are critical.

Documents, in various forms, still exist and are becoming harder and harder to manage, or their appropriate management is simply being ignored. Over twenty years ago, physical documents were simple, but today, the document can be a myriad of things: an email, a PDF, and image, a text message, a chat stream, a social media post, and even more.

This book provides a strategic model for evaluating an organization's end-to-end document management process, developing a road map to improve it, and measuring those improvements.

Overall

A Formula for Innovation

Vince Lombardi once said, "It is time for us to all stand and cheer for the doer, the achiever--the one who recognizes the challenge and does something about it." The thing that differentiates between a "human being" and a "human doing" is our ability to act in innovative ways in the face of adversity.

Plato, in his work, *The Republic*, said, "Necessity is the mother of invention." Necessity may be the mother of invention, but innovation is the foundation of overall positive change, and change requires more than simple necessity for it to occur.

Between the two--innovation and invention-- there are arguably common themes. In this book, explain that an actual formula exists for true innovative thought. This formula, not easily defined, is made up of several variables.

The Encyclopedia defines innovation as the introduction of new ideas, goods, services, and practices, which are intended to be useful. The main driver for innovation is often the courage and energy to better the world. When you take a more in-depth view of innovation, especially regarding invention, there are numerous variables that impact the activity.

A Formula for Innovation explores and explains the formula for true innovative thought, how to use it and how it can influence your organization and business.

Made in the USA
Middletown, DE
30 April 2019